Boards That Love Fundraising

Boards That Love Fundraising

A How-to Guide
for Your Board

Robert M. Zimmerman
and Ann W. Lehman

JOSSEY-BASS
A Wiley Imprint
www.josseybass.com

Published by Jossey-Bass
A Wiley Imprint
989 Market Street, San Francisco, CA 94103-1741   www.josseybass.com

The materials that appear in this book (except those for which reprint permission must be obtained from the primary sources) may be reproduced for educational/training activities. We do, however, require that the following statement appear on all reproductions:

Boards That Love Fundraising: A How-to Guide for Your Board by Robert M. Zimmerman and Ann W. Lehman
   Copyright © 2004 by John Wiley & Sons, Inc.

This free permission is limited to the reproduction of material for educational/training events. Systematic or large-scale reproduction or distribution (more than one hundred copies per year)—or inclusion of items in publications for sale—may be done only with prior written permission. Also, reproduction on computer disk or by any other electronic means requires prior written permission. Requests to the Publisher for permission should be addressed to the Permissions Department, John Wiley & Sons, Inc., 111 River Street, Hoboken, NJ 07030, (201) 748-6011, fax (201) 748-6008, e-mail: permcoordinator@wiley.com.

Jossey-Bass books and products are available through most bookstores. To contact Jossey-Bass directly call our Customer Care Department within the U.S. at 800-956-7739, outside the U.S. at 317-572-3986 or fax 317-572-4002.

Jossey-Bass also publishes its books in a variety of electronic formats. Some content that appears in print may not be available in electronic books.

Library of Congress Cataloging-in-Publication Data
Zimmerman, Robert M., 1947–
   Boards that love fundraising : a how-to guide for your board / by
Robert M. Zimmerman and Ann W. Lehman.
       p. cm.
Includes bibliographical references and index.
   ISBN 0-7879-6812-9 (alk. paper)
   1. Fund raising. 2. Nonprofit organizations—Finance. I. Lehman, Ann
W. II. Title.
   HG177.Z547 2004
   658.15'224—dc22
                                                                        2003024913

Printed in the United States of America

FIRST EDITION

PB Printing   10 9 8 7 6 5 4 3 2 1

Contents

Exercises

About the Authors

ROBERT (BOB) ZIMMERMAN and **ANN W. LEHMAN** lived through and were influenced heavily by the idealism of the 1960s. While less naïve now, they have not lost their enthusiasm for creating a just and healthy world. Their work today provides nonprofit organizations with pragmatic action plans to guarantee operational effectiveness and financial success.

Bob Zimmerman, fundraising specialist and president of Zimmerman Lehman, has more than thirty years of experience in the areas of fundraising, board and volunteer training and development, and executive search. A 1969 graduate of Antioch College, with a master's degree in political science from the University of Michigan, he started his career at a large community counseling program in Boston as a grantwriter (in the good old Nixon days, when federal money was easily found). He has been the director of development at a variety of nonprofit organizations on both coasts, including an independent living center for physically disabled people in Los Angeles and a national public interest law office in San Francisco.

In 1988, he founded Zimmerman Lehman, a consulting firm whose motto is "forging futures for nonprofits." The firm specializes in fundraising, organizational development, and executive search exclusively on behalf of nonprofits. He has consulted with numerous organizations both large and small in every area of nonprofit endeavor. He has taught thousands of individuals the art and science of fundraising, in particular helping trainees overcome their fears. He has conducted his renowned interactive workshops throughout the United States and in Europe on such topics as Zimmerman's rules of fundraising, major donor solicitation, grantseeking, hiring top-notch executive staff, and capital campaigns.

He has served on the board of directors of the Golden Gate Chapter of the Association of Fundraising Professionals (AFP) and has cochaired AFP's

"Fundraising Day" in San Francisco. He is the author of the newsletter *The Zimmerman Telegram* and its more modern incarnation, *ZimNotes*, an e-newsletter on fundraising started in 1997. He has also written the training manuals *Grantseeking: A Step-by-Step Approach*; *Major Donors: The Key to Successful Fundraising*; and *Maximum Dollars: The 12 Rules of Fundraising*; he is the coauthor (with partner Ann W. Lehman) of *The Effective Nonprofit Board: Responsibilities and Recruitment*.

Ann W. Lehman, lawyer, planning specialist, executive coach, trainer, and policy expert, has worked in the public interest arena for more than twenty-five years. She brings her wide experience as executive director, activist, senior policy analyst, consultant, trainer, facilitator, board member, and coach to the Zimmerman Lehman consultancy. She received her B.A. from Rutgers University in New Jersey in 1974 and her J.D. from Northwestern School of Law in Portland, Oregon, in 1978. Immediately after law school, she supervised a storefront public interest law center in Portland geared to senior citizens. She has directed an alternative bar association in New York City; worked as a senior policy analyst on women, girls, and human rights; and was the executive director of a public interest law office specializing in issues affecting seniors.

She joined Zimmerman Lehman in 1991 and has consulted and taught workshops in such areas as strategic and programmatic planning, board responsibilities and recruitment, fundraising, leadership, advocacy, office management, human rights, work-life issues, and sexual harassment. She has facilitated numerous conferences and retreats nationwide. She is coauthor of Zimmerman Lehman 's book *The Effective Nonprofit Board: Responsibilities and Recruitment* and webmistress of Zimmerman Lehman's website, www.zimmerman-lehman.com.

She has also developed a sexual harassment prevention program and worked extensively implementing the Convention on the Elimination of All Forms of Discrimination Against Women (CEDAW), a human rights treaty for women and girls in San Francisco. She has authored a survey and report on work-life options and a major report on girls in San Francisco. Ann also chairs her neighborhood association and is a member of the El Cerrito Economic Development Board.

Bob Zimmerman and Ann Lehman, also life partners, live in El Cerrito, California, with their son, Gabe Z. Lehman, and their dog, Stella.

Acknowledgements

WITHOUT A DOUBT the real heroes of this book are the many individuals who work at nonprofit organizations and dedicate their lives to ensuring we live in a healthy and equitable world. In particular, we would like to thank our client staff members who grapple daily to balance the variety of needs of their organizations, board members who volunteer their time and treasure, and donors who believe in the value of our clients' work. While we preach in this book that organizations need to be more "businesslike," we know that the "bottom line" is not a measure of success and that the many individuals who work so hard are not doing so for the lucrative salaries or benefits that nonprofits provide. We hope after reading this book that that will change!

There are many challenges in writing a book. As both professional and personal partners, we would like to acknowledge each other for having completed this book with our relationship still intact, our different strengths recognized and our sense of humor revitalized. This would not have been possible without the assistance of Rinat Fried, who provided so much help and good cheer as we prepared the first draft.

We would also like to thank our parents and families for their openness about the issue of money and for their belief in us as successful human beings.

Introduction

WE CANNOT PRAISE TOO HIGHLY the contributions that nonprofit organizations make to the welfare of communities throughout the United States. The "third sector" (after for-profit companies and the government) creates millions of jobs and offers services that benefit millions more; nonprofit board members, staff, and other volunteers are to be congratulated for their Herculean efforts. We are thankful also for this nation's longstanding philanthropic tradition. Whether the economy is good or bad, whether the prevailing political winds are liberal or conservative, Americans can be depended upon to make handsome contributions to organizations amounting to hundreds of billions of dollars annually.

The money is out there, even in tough economic times. For example, according to *Giving USA*, a publication of the American Association of Fundraising Counsel's Trust for Philanthropy, more than $241 billion was given to 1.4 million charitable organizations in 2002. This represents 2.3 percent of the U.S. gross domestic product and constitutes an increase in absolute dollars over 2001.[1] What is remarkable here is that 2002 was a very poor year economically in the United States, yet people continued to give.

If so much money is potentially available, why are so many organizations suffering from too little revenue? The answer has nothing to do with the fickleness of the public, "donor fatigue," or the controversial nature of certain nonprofit activities. The answer, quite simply, is that board and staff members don't ask for money effectively, they don't ask often enough, and sometimes they don't ask—period. Every year, billions of dollars that could be invested in the nonprofit sector are lost because organizations aren't asking properly.

Many board members, volunteers, and staff members view fundraising as "genteel begging" rather than as creating opportunities for citizens to invest in successful enterprises through philanthropic contributions. This book is grounded in the conviction that nonprofits are business enterprises similar in many important respects to for-profit enterprises. As a member of a nonprofit board, you should make sure that your organization is carefully managed, is fulfilling its mission, and has sufficient financial resources at its command to implement current and future programs.

You can also learn to be an effective "salesperson" for your organization. Although you sell concepts (for example, a healthier environment, better-educated children, or cultural enrichment), not products, you are a salesperson nonetheless. In soliciting new prospects, cultivating donors, and diversifying your funding base, your fundraising job as a board member is to satisfy the "customer" (that is, the donor) without misrepresenting the work of your organization. Donors should be proud to invest in your organization!

As nonprofit consultants with decades of experience working with all types of organizations, from small start-ups to large nationwide enterprises, we cringe when we hear the oft-repeated lament, "I was told when I joined this board that the one thing I wouldn't have to do was fundraising!" In fact, the board of directors is the single most important element in nonprofit fundraising. An enthusiastic, well-trained, and well-connected board guarantees fundraising success. An indifferent or hostile board with no connections to money, no determination to forge those connections, and no interest in learning fundraising techniques gravely compromise your organization's ability to achieve its goals. As a member of a nonprofit board, you can and must help ensure your organization's financial well-being.

This book is divided into five chapters. Chapter One, "What Every Board Member Needs to Know to Start Fundraising," explains your fundraising responsibilities as a board member and presents information on board structure and its impact on raising money. Chapter Two, "Fundraising Rules Underlying Successful Appeals," explains to you the concepts that enable you to ask for money effectively and fearlessly. In Chapter Three, "The Board's Role in Specific Fundraising Activities," we describe in detail the variety of ways that nonprofits raise funds and the board's role in each area. Chapter Four, "Effective Board Recruitment," steers you away from "anecdotal" board recruitment and toward a rational recruitment policy designed to draw folks to your board who will be of the greatest assistance with fundraising and other board endeavors. Chapter Five, "Primed for Fundraising," deals with the critically important issues of fundraising planning, staffing, evaluation, and working with consultants.

If you are new to the world of fundraising, we are confident that, having completed this volume and done the exercises, you will understand your fundraising role as a board member and be "rarin' to go" to corral that first gift. If you are a board member seasoned in particular aspects of fundraising, we trust that this book will alert you to new areas in which you can play a vitally important role and hone your fundraising skills.

A Word on the Exercises

The exercises in this book are designed to give you a hands-on appreciation of fundraising concepts and techniques. Some exercises are role plays; others offer the opportunity for discussion about your organization's development efforts; still others provide the means to plan for a fiscally healthy future.

Most of the exercises require a leader who acts as the facilitator. This might be your board chair, your development committee chair, a staff member, or a consultant. In some exercises, we have listed questions for participants to consider. We encourage each person to write down his or her answers prior to beginning the discussion; this will prove more fruitful than simply jumping in.

Exercises are of course designed for your board of directors (or a subgroup such as the development committee), but we hope that the executive director and development director will also be included as appropriate. Most of the exercises (other than the role plays) can also be completed by individual board or staff members if it is inconvenient to assemble the full board or development committee; simply brainstorm with yourself and write down your responses to the questions. A few exercises involve consideration of confidential information; in these cases, we have given specific instructions concerning who should participate in the discussions. Finally, we have included the amount of time that we anticipate each exercise will take. This varies with the number of people participating.

A word on terminology: since, in the nonprofit world, the terms *fundraising* and *development* are used interchangeably, we also use both words to mean the same thing.

Note

1. *Giving USA*, a publication of the AAFRC Trust for Philanthropy, researched and written by the Center on Philanthropy at Indiana University. http://aafrc.org/

Chapter 1

What Every Board Member Needs to Know to Start Fundraising

SINCE YOU ARE READING this book, we can assume at the very least that you appreciate the importance of board members' involvement in your organization's development efforts. Although not the board's only responsibility, fundraising is often what causes the most trepidation on the part of both new and seasoned members. A few of you may be wildly enthusiastic about the prospect of talking to potential donors and convincing them to invest in your organization; most of you probably find the prospect daunting. To place fundraising in proper perspective, let's take a look at your overall responsibilities as a board member.

The Five Responsibilities of a Nonprofit Board

Nonprofit board members have five major responsibilities:

1. To ensure sound planning and policies (write the mission and vision statements; make sure that programs accord with the mission)

2. To ensure good management (evaluate, hire, and if necessary fire the executive director; review personnel policies)

3. To ensure sound resources and financial dealings (assist with fundraising and public relations; guarantee financial accountability)

4. To ensure compliance with legal requirements (file required papers and act as a trustee/fiduciary; comply with bylaws)

5. To ensure good governance (conduct a periodic board self-evaluation; keep minutes; recruit new members; update bylaws as appropriate)

Being an effective board member means more than just showing up at meetings; it requires staying informed and asking difficult questions, participating in planning and policy making, ensuring a sound financial footing, and monitoring and evaluating the management and governance of the organization.

Specific Board Fundraising Responsibilities

A critically important part of good board management is ensuring the availability of adequate funds. What specifically should nonprofit board members do in this regard? As a nonprofit board member, you have four fundraising responsibilities:

1. To make a financial contribution to the extent of your capacity. Some board members can make only a token gift annually; others can give $5 million. Each of you should make a "stretch" gift every year, regardless of the specific amount. Other funders—particularly foundations and major donors—will consider making contributions only if everyone on the board has made a capacity gift. It is much easier to ask for money if you have put your money where your mouth is!

2. To solicit contributions from your friends, relatives, and colleagues. The most important reason that a person makes his or her first contribution to a nonprofit organization is that the right person asks. You should be prepared to approach the individuals on your Christmas, Chanukah, Kwanzaa, Ramadan, or Solstice card list on behalf of your organization. These approaches may be for a direct mail contribution, a seat at a special event, a major gift, or a planned gift.

3. To assist with recruiting new members to your board of directors who have the clout and connections to ensure the success of the fundraising effort. To achieve critical mass when it comes to fundraising, your board must contain at least a few people of means who have the ability to make sizeable contributions and the desire to "put the arm" on friends and colleagues. Peer-to-peer fundraising is the name of the game.

4. To oversee your organization's fundraising efforts. As a board member, it is not your responsibility to write grant proposals or enter donor information in the database (unless there is no staff). You are responsible, however, for making sure that your organization is pursuing funds by every appropriate means. The board mandates preparation of a written fundraising plan and reviews fundraising activities periodically to ensure timely and comprehensive implementation of the plan.

As fundraising consultants, we have worked with thousands of board members at hundreds of nonprofit organizations, and it is rare indeed for anyone to say, "Naturally those are our responsibilities! Lead on!" We face instead a variety of concerns about each responsibility.

Making a Financial Contribution to the Extent of Your Capacity

First, with reference to making their own financial contributions, typical objections and complaints voiced by board members include:

"I give my time, and that's more valuable than money!"

"What difference can my small gift make to a huge nonprofit like this?"

"I serve on three nonprofit boards. How can I contribute to each one?"

We certainly appreciate the time that board members donate, but this doesn't replace money. If you are a consultant in the field of public health who bills at $350 an hour and you spend five hours per month on nonprofit board work, this does not equate to $1,750, because $1,750 does not appear magically in the organization's bank account. Of course volunteer hours matter—but so does money.

If your organization has an annual budget of $10 million, why should anyone care about your contribution of $250? Two reasons: first, the huge majority of that $10 million may be restricted to particular projects, and your $250 unrestricted contribution is therefore extremely helpful in meeting such mundane expenses as utility bills and purchasing copy paper. Second, your modest contribution is vitally important philanthropic advertising. Prospective major individual donors are likely to ask solicitors from the board if they have made contributions themselves. The right answer? "Yes, and my gift was the largest I've ever made to a nonprofit organization," or "Yes, and it was a real stretch, but that's how much this organization means to me." Some nonprofit board members serve on more than one board, and their largesse is therefore spread thin. We appreciate this problem and ask only that board members do the best they can to bolster each organization's revenues.

Soliciting Contributions from Your Friends, Relatives, and Colleagues

The very idea of asking friends for contributions fills many board members with fear and loathing. When we conduct board fundraising trainings, we always ask this question: "How many of you would rather ask a stranger for a large gift than a friend?" Inevitably, the majority of the folks in the room raise their hands. Our response? "Ladies and gentlemen, you're going to have to get over it."

Why? Because the most important tactical issue in fundraising is access. How do you gain access to folks with money and the desire to help a worthy organization? You clearly do not have access to strangers; sending a letter to Mr. and Ms. Dinero on Plush Drive requesting a contribution is pointless unless someone in your organization knows Mr. and Ms. Dinero personally. We understand that not every board member has well-heeled friends and colleagues, but everyone knows folks who could make modest contributions. The folks whom you know will at the very least grant you an audience or be willing to read a request letter to which you have appended a personal note. As we discuss later in this book, you must learn to overcome the fears that keep you from asking your intimates for contributions.

Recruiting New Members with Clout and Connections to Your Board of Directors

Board members at small- and medium-sized organizations are often reluctant to invite folks with money and connections onto their board. This reluctance is equal parts fear of being intimidated and what we term "reverse chic." Current board members worry that someone with money and clout will so intimidate them that they will never say another word at a board meeting. Conversely, they honestly believe that a person of means could not possibly relate to the work of their organization!

For example, one client, a small modern dance company in a large city on the West Coast, called us for a board consultation. The dance company was five years old at the time of our meeting; its initial funding included grants from foundations and government agencies, as well as modest contributions from local businesses. The board was made up of dancers, choreographers, and friends of the artistic director. The grants and contributions were drying up, and they needed advice on what to do next.

We suggested that they needed to raise funds from individuals; to do so, it was vitally important to expand their board. "How about asking the manager of the bank branch at which you do business to join your board?" we suggested. Their reaction spoke volumes about intimidation and reverse chic: "What?" said one of the current board members. "What could a bank manager possibly know about modern dance?"

There are two issues here. First, the bank manager is not being asked to choreograph a production; what matters is that he or she cares a great deal about dance. More important, to dismiss the idea of a banker serving on the dance company's board is to deny the board a powerful fundraising ally.

Overseeing Your Organization's Fundraising Efforts

Finally, board members are often uncomfortable in the role of overseer of the development effort. They would rather cede this responsibility to staff. "Thank heavens we've hired our first development director," board members often say. "No more fundraising for us!" In fact, a good development director makes your board work hard and consistently at fundraising. In addition, the development director and executive director look to the board for guidance in planning and implementing all facets of your fundraising effort.

As discussed in Chapter Five, the board should commission a written fundraising plan, to be prepared either by the development director or a consultant. The plan gives your organization its fundraising marching orders for three years. As a board member, it is your responsibility to review the plan periodically and interview staff to determine whether all necessary steps have been taken to implement it.

A Healthy Board

Healthy organizations raise more money than their ailing counterparts. At Zimmerman Lehman, we believe board health depends upon an effective chairperson, functioning committees, and stable operations. The chairperson is an informed and enthusiastic leader. He or she chairs board meetings, meets regularly with the executive director to review operations, and stays in touch with committee chairs to make sure that committees are operating smoothly (more on this later). The board chair is also responsible for soliciting financial contributions from all board members.

An effective nonprofit board relies on standing committees to do the lion's share of the work. Every member of your board should be responsible for serving on at least one committee:

- *Executive:* sets the board agenda and makes emergency decisions between board meetings on behalf of the entire board
- *Finance:* oversees fiscal operations
- *Nominating:* reviews current board composition, makes recommendations concerning the background of new members, and interviews prospective members
- *Personnel:* prepares personnel policies and evaluates the executive director
- *Program:* monitors program operations and makes recommendations to the executive director
- *Public relations:* gives the organization a higher profile in the community by speaking at appropriate public gatherings and serving as contact people with print and electronic media
- *Membership:* those organizations whose members directly elect the board of directors—a small but hardy minority—should also have a board membership committee to determine such things as categories of membership and requisite dues

- And of course, *fundraising:* in one form or another, every board member contributes to your organization's financial well-being, though certain members have a greater flair for, or interest in, the art and science of solicitation; these individuals belong on your board's fundraising committee

The job of the fundraising committee is to provide expert advice and assistance to both staff and board. For example, if your organization plans to conduct a direct mail campaign, fundraising committee members should meet with executive staff to discuss the overall concept for the campaign and brainstorm with staff about appropriate mailing lists. Committee members should not draft direct mail copy—that is the responsibility of the staff or a consultant—but should offer oversight and support to ensure a successful campaign.

It is important to note, however, that the entire fundraising committee is not responsible for every fundraising activity. A labor-intensive project such as a special event requires an ad hoc committee made up of some members of the fundraising committee and other volunteers who are particularly interested in the glitz and glamour of an event (and who bring important skills to the table). The fundraising committee is responsible for spearheading your organization's annual evaluation of the fundraising effort. Committee members must therefore be sufficiently aware of all facets of your fundraising operation to be able to prepare a useful and comprehensive evaluation.

Finally, an effective board must operate soundly and consistently. The board must meet often enough to tackle important issues; annual board meetings simply do not afford this opportunity. A sufficient number of members must show up at every meeting to constitute a quorum, and minutes and other materials must be distributed to members at least a week before the meeting. The executive committee—which, as indicated, draws up the agenda—should indicate a time limit for each agenda item. If the board goes beyond the allotted time, a motion must be made and passed to extend the time for that item. We highly recommend the use of Robert's Rules of Order to ensure that meetings proceed expeditiously. Though it might appear that we have strayed from the topic of fundraising, we have discovered in our work with nonprofits that happy board members raise money. A board that operates with intelligence and dispatch keeps its members happy.

Advisory Boards

Some organizations have done well with a fundraising entity separate from the board of directors (variously termed an "advisory council," "advisory board," or "friends of the organization"). A group of this sort usually comprises individuals who are not interested in board membership but are excited about adopting the organization as their "pet charity," or lending their name to the development effort. For example, a disabled advocacy program in southern California convened an advisory council made up of Hollywood personalities who were not interested in membership on the board of directors but who believed in the importance of the organization's work. The advisory council has raised many millions of dollars on behalf of this nonprofit through such special events as dinners and auctions.

Three words of warning, however, about convening a separate advisory council. First, the council requires staff time to keep members apprised of meetings and current issues, and staff time may already be in very short supply. Second, a person may be recruited to the council who would really rather get his or her hands dirty by serving on the board of directors. Don't assume that a famous and wealthy person wouldn't be interested in membership on your board of directors! Third—and most important—the existence of something like a fundraising advisory council or friends committee does not absolve the board of directors of its fundraising responsibilities. A separate fundraising group is an appealing add-on, but the board of directors remains vital to the development effort.

Campaigns

It is important to understand that fundraising should be done within the context of a campaign. Why is this important? Because episodic fundraising (what we call "let's put on a play" fundraising) doesn't work. A direct mail campaign here, a special event there simply won't be effective. The best fundraising is done under the umbrella of a campaign.

Each campaign has a beginning and ending date, a dollar goal, and a schedule of activities. Also, every board member, staff member, and other volunteer in the campaign has marching orders describing exactly what he or she is responsible for, plus the anticipated date of completion. As a board member, you must be clear about what each campaign entails before you can do effective fundraising. We highlight a few of the most common kinds of campaign here, but any fundraising campaign should follow these guidelines.

Annual Campaign

As its name implies, the annual campaign is carried out every year to raise funds for your organization's general operating expenses and for particular projects. We strongly recommend that all fundraising other than capital and endowment campaigns (discussed later) be placed under the aegis of the annual campaign. In fundraising, each activity should fit into an overall scheme: the direct mail campaign that you conduct in January has a direct impact on the special event that you do in June and the telephone solicitation that you run in October. All are part of the annual campaign.

What you as a board member are "selling" when raising funds for the annual campaign is your love for and excitement about your organization. Certainly you should be armed with relevant statistics and good stories, but what closes the sale is your personal commitment to your organization's goals and programs. As a board member, you are responsible for overseeing timely implementation of the annual campaign and for the particular activities described in Chapter Three.

Capital Campaign

A capital campaign raises funds for a building purchase, building renovation, land acquisition, or purchase of a large piece of equipment. In our experience, a capital campaign attracts money more easily than an annual campaign for two reasons: it is tangible ("My $20,000 helped pay for this classroom") and it offers donors the opportunity to have their name placed on a building, wall, or individual computer.

A successful capital campaign depends upon committed and enthusiastic board members. Management of the capital campaign is the responsibility of the capital campaign committee (see "Campaign Committees" later), which is composed of board members, staff members, and other volunteers who are passionately committed to the work of the organization. A capital campaign may last for as little as one year or as long as six years or more, and it depends on a combination of funding strategies.

Endowment Campaign

An endowment is a sum of money whose principal may not be touched by your nonprofit; only the interest generated from the principal is available to be spent. Donors who give to an endowment campaign are excited about building a corpus of funding that will generate income for your organization for many years to come.

If your organization is relatively new, we do not recommend establishing an endowment. You must demonstrate a significant record of achievement if you are to convince a prospective donor to make an endowment investment. Also, many donors want to see their money put into play immediately. An endowment is not attractive to these folks.

If on the other hand your organization boasts an impressive record of achievement, and if you can line up a donor who is prepared to make a very large gift, you should certainly try to get an endowment program off the ground. With appropriate nurturing, your endowment corpus will grow, and the resulting interest represents significant organizational income.

Campaign Committees

The overall responsibility for your campaign lies with the campaign committee, which is made up of board members, the executive director, the development director, and other volunteers (this latter category might include ex-staff, ex-board, donors, clients, or community volunteers).

The committee sets dollar goals and approves a campaign theme and timetable. Members are responsible for asking for gifts. The committee interviews consultants or employees who will staff the campaign. Staff responsibilities include preparing a calendar and written materials for the committee, scheduling meetings, conducting research, and reminding volunteers of their commitment to the campaign.

The campaign committee should include a variety of volunteers who will ensure the campaign's success. For example, the capital campaign committee responsible for building a health clinic should include (in addition to appropriate board members) doctors and other medical staff who can movingly describe the importance of the clinic. Among the details that the committee should address are these:

- Developing a campaign timetable and budget

- Developing a theme or "case" for the campaign; the committee must explain the particulars of the campaign and why it will improve your organization's services to clients

- Brainstorming to determine who the best prospects are and how much to request from each

- Determining the "naming opportunities"; if you are purchasing or constructing a building, how much will it cost a donor to have his or her name on a room? a wing? the entire building?

- Developing appropriate recognition opportunities for those donors whose gifts don't qualify them for naming status

- Making sure the staff prepares comprehensive materials for solicitors, including research reports on prospects and "crib sheets" that solicitors (askers) can turn to for vital campaign details

- Deciding whether and when to hold a campaign kickoff event

- Thanking donors promptly and imaginatively

We cannot emphasize too strongly the importance of each committee member asking for gifts. The success of your campaign rests on skilled and determined solicitors. The committee must therefore schedule training sessions that will, as we explain in Chapter Two, help members overcome their fear of asking and equip them with the skills to ask convincingly.

Chapter 2

Fundraising Rules Underlying Successful Appeals

FUNDRAISING DOES NOT OCCUR in a vacuum. If as a board member you are to solicit contributions effectively and consistently, you need to understand the concepts that underpin successful fundraising. For example, a successful direct mail campaign depends on the board understanding that *people give money to people.* This makes it easier to enlist the board's help in appending personal notes on letters to friends and colleagues. If your board hopes to solicit major individual gifts, you must understand that *fundraising is done from the donor's perspective.* Getting the prospect talking about his or her interests and concerns paves the way to getting a big gift.

Zimmerman Lehman developed these rules after many years of providing training and consultation to hundreds of nonprofit organizations. Board and staff members who understand and apply these rules are well on the way to raising the money needed to maintain and expand valuable efforts.

Programming Determines Funding

Before you can begin to raise money, you must know what you are raising the money for. What are the current and future programs for which your organization is seeking funds? If you don't have a strategic plan, you need to develop one, or at a minimum a comprehensive, current mission statement to guide and direct you in your fundraising efforts. (*See Exercise 1.*)

Funders particularly like to hear that you have thought about every detail, have a plan of action, and now simply need the funds to move forward (which is exactly what a for-profit company must do when it tries to raise capital). You should address these questions:

- What does your organization want to do in the world?
- What are your goals?
- How do you intend to implement them?
- What will it cost?
- Where will you find the money?

Do not make the mistake of first examining what funders are interested in and then designing your programs to align with their interests. This is tempting, but it's the first step on the road to ruin. An organization that has a history of chasing the money often ends up as a pastiche of special projects, few of which accord with the organization's original mission.

Take, for example, an after-school program whose mission is to help boost the math and science achievements of junior high school girls. One day the director of the project is approached by a grantor seeking to fund a sports project for girls. The executive director is faced with a dilemma: accepting the grant would bring much-needed money to the organization, but the project is not in accordance with the organization's mission. She turns to her board members, who tell her to resist the temptation, knowing that the new grant would distract staff from its mission and possibly undermine the agency's core programs.

Mission Statement

Of course, not all funding opportunities are as black-and-white as in this example. Your mission statement and strategic plan are the rudders that keep your organization on course in developing programs and securing donations. Every nonprofit needs a concise and comprehensive mission statement; a clear sense of mission and direction inspires staff, board, and volunteers.

It is the job of the board of directors to write the mission statement and amend it should circumstances so dictate. The mission of the organization is the reason for its existence; therefore the mission statement should answer these questions:

- What need are you meeting?
- Whom do you serve?
- What are your geographic boundaries?
- What problems are you attempting to solve?
- Through what methods and programs do you make the effort to solve these problems?

Here's an example of the mission statement of a statewide foster youth empowerment organization:

> *California Youth Connection, an organization that is guided, focused, and driven by current and former foster youth, promotes the participation of foster youth in policy development and legislative change to improve the foster care system. California Youth Connection strives to work with decision makers to improve social work practice and child welfare policy.*[1]

The purpose of the mission statement is twofold: to articulate your goals for all to see and to determine whether new program ideas fall within the scope of your organization. If the California Youth Connection executive director approached her board with plans to initiate a program on behalf of adoptive infants, this would fly in the face of the mission statement. The board of directors would then have to do one of two things: reject the new program because it does not fit within the mission statement, or amend the mission statement to include the new program. As the folks with ultimate responsibility for overseeing the organization, board members must review the mission statement annually to ensure its continued appropriateness.

Strategic Planning

If a mission statement is a concise treatment of your organization's vision and values, a strategic plan is the game plan for helping your organization achieve that vision and manifest those values through its programs.

A strategic plan is crucial to fundraising. Before your organization is ready to conduct effective fundraising, you must know where you are going in the next three years and how you intend to get there. In final form, the strategic plan includes your organization's vision, mission, goals, objectives, and specific activities in the next five years. Your fundraising pitches will be compelling and credible thanks to the focus and specificity of your plan.

For each organization you should have the elements seen in Exhibit 2.1.

Getting People to Ask

Even in tough economic times, there is more than enough philanthropic money to go around. Between 2000 and the end of 2002, for example, when the U.S. economy was perilously close to deflation, Americans gave away in excess of $672 billion to charity. Do the math: can 1.5 million nonprofits survive on an average of $224 billion per year?[2] We think they can. Your principal concern, then, is not whether donors will contribute; it is whether you can secure the consistent, imaginative support of board members, staff members, and other volunteers in planning campaigns and asking for money.

EXHIBIT 2.1

Vision

The broadest and brightest view of the future

Mission

The What? How? Who? in a few sentences

Goals

Broad aim or purpose

Objectives

Quantifiable measures to achieve goals

Tasks

Activities required to achieve objectives

EXERCISE 1

Programming Determines Funding

Participants: This exercise requires a facilitator and can be done with the entire board and executive staff.

The facilitator picks one project currently offered by your organization or being considered for the near future. Here are questions to consider:

- How does this project relate to your mission?
- How and why was the project initiated?
  - Is it because the client community demanded it?
  - Is it because staff or the board thought it would serve the needs of the client community?
  - Is it because it is something we've always done?
  - Is it because we knew it was fundable?
- Is this project included in your strategic plan?

Think next about what this project might look like if sufficient funding were available. (This is a strategic planning exercise and is included here to point out how much of what you do is restricted by current available funding. This book is about helping you develop the skills to create new funding streams.)

Time: Twenty-five to thirty-five minutes

You Are Not Inferior

Many board (and staff) members suffer from a terrible inferiority complex. They assume that fundraising is a process of going on bended knee to the donor, asking for the least possible amount of money, and being graced from on high with a contribution.

No! Fundraising means getting in people's faces (politely) to let them know that, if they are not giving to your organization—and giving a significant amount—they are missing an important opportunity. You should make every effort to limit use of such words as *gift, contribution*, and *donation* and instead think of fundraising as an investment in a successful community enterprise.

As noted earlier, being a board member of a nonprofit is not much different from being a board member of a corporation. Board members and fundraisers are salespeople: you are selling the benefits that will accrue to the community thanks to the donor's investment. We sell concepts (a cleaner environment, a healthier population, better-educated children), not products, but we are salespeople nonetheless. A donor's decision about whether to give and how much to give is no different from his or her decision to invest money in corporate stock. When an individual "invests" in your organization, the "return" is the benefit your organization bestows on the community—be it cultural, environmental, educational, health-related, or in any of a variety of other disciplines.

Your organization provides a service to the community, and philanthropists pay for that service. It's a *quid pro quo* arrangement, not tin-cup begging. Keeping this principle in mind enables you to raise money as boldly as any business seeking to grow its revenue through sales and investments.

It is also vitally important that your organization ask for money in as many ways as are appropriate. In the next chapter, we review in detail the fundraising techniques available to nonprofits. It is the rare organization that is raising money in every way available to it. Whether it is solicitation of gifts by mail, special events, proposals to foundations, fees for services, or any of a host of other avenues, chances are your organization is missing at least one opportunity and probably more.

You Need Not Fear Asking for Money

Most board members fear fundraising. All too often the executive director or development director accedes to this fear. Board members are relieved of their fundraising duties, and staff members do what they can to solicit small foundation grants and modest individual contributions. Big gifts?

They never make it onto the organization's radar screen, because the people who should be doing the asking—the board members—fail to pick up the ball.

The bad news: the typical organization fails to identify all of its major donor prospects. Some don't identify any. As a result, individuals who could give thousands or tens of thousands of dollars are sent direct mail letters requesting contributions of $100 or less. The good news: hundreds of millions of dollars could be gained every year by the simple decision to pursue major gifts.

Please understand first that, in asking for a contribution to the nonprofit on whose board you serve, you are not asking for a personal loan. Rather, you are so enthusiastic about the work of your organization that you want to give your friends the opportunity to participate in the life of the organization by making a contribution.

Some years ago, a member of our consulting firm accompanied the board president of a legal aid program on a solicitation visit to the managing partner of a large local law firm. The board president and the consultant described the good work of the legal aid program and emphasized the importance of support from law firms. The managing partner listened politely to the pitch and replied: "Thank you for your presentation. I love the work that legal aid does. To tell you the truth, I'd much rather work for legal aid than for this stuffy downtown firm. Unfortunately, I have a big mortgage and two daughters in college; considering the salary you could pay me, I couldn't possibly work for you. And I'm so busy I don't even have time to volunteer at legal aid. The least I can do is give you some money!"

The managing partner wanted to demonstrate her respect and affection for legal aid. She couldn't do so by working, or even volunteering, there, but she had an option: a financial contribution. Money in this context is not an end; it is a means to connect with an organization that excites the donor's imagination.

Fear and Loathing About Fundraising

Let's look at the fears that keep us from raising funds. In our experience, the most common fears are rejection, embarrassment, and the *quid pro quo*. Rejection is the fear we encounter most frequently: "If I ask a colleague for a contribution and he or she says 'no,' then, like the wicked witch in *The Wizard of Oz*, I will melt into the floor, never to be heard from again."

In convincing you not to fear rejection, it's useful to think of a vacuum cleaner salesperson going door-to-door. If that salesperson goes to thirty-five houses and sells ten vacuum cleaners, was that a good day or a bad day? It was a fine day, even though twenty-five of the thirty-five prospects said no! The fact that many people will say no to your solicitations is not the point. What matters is this: if you do appropriate donor research and approach prospects intelligently and respectfully, enough of them will say yes to make your efforts worthwhile.

What about embarrassment? We noted earlier that the most important tactical consideration in fundraising is access to the prospective donor, yet most folks are terrified to ask intimates for contributions. Why do we fear asking the people who are closest to us? Some folks think that fundraising is embarrassing, obnoxious, and invasive; asking for a contribution, they believe, is trading unethically on a friendship.

It's odd, isn't it? We live in a capitalist society, yet the most embarrassing subject in our society is money. Many of us were taught as children that it is bad form to inquire how much someone makes, or to estimate how much someone is worth. Board members have transferred this prohibition into the fundraising realm—where it does not belong. Again, we are giving people the opportunity to feel good by helping an organization that is doing important work. We mustn't let embarrassment about money get in the way.

The third fear we often encounter is the *quid pro quo*: "If I ask a friend for a contribution to my organization, what's to stop him or her from ask-

---

EXERCISE 2A

Fundraising Fears

Participants: This exercise requires a facilitator and should be done with the entire board.

At a board meeting, the facilitator asks this question: "How many people in this room would consider it fun to sit across the table from a friend and ask for a contribution to our organization?" Trust us: most people will not raise their hands. If anyone does raise a hand, ask why he or she thinks this would be fun. Ask the others if they agree. For those who did not raise their hands, ask them to write down their fears of asking, collect them, and summarize on a flipchart. Put a check next to each fear for each additional person who shares that fear.

Review each fear; discuss as a group and attempt to defuse it by referring to the material in Chapter Two, looking at your own cultural biases around money, and developing a group response for each fear. If you have a large group, you can divide members into subgroups of three or four. Assign one fear to each group and ask group members to discuss the fear and develop a group response. Have one person report each group's response to the full meeting and write them on a flipchart.

Time: Twenty-five to thirty-five minutes

ing me for a contribution to his or her favorite organization six months from now?" The answer? Nothing at all. But talk about a poor reason for not doing the fundraising! Your friend may or may not give to your organization; you may or may not give to your friend's. The sun will come up tomorrow. In our many years working with nonprofits, we have never heard of a friendship destroyed by Person A asking Person B for a philanthropic contribution. If you—the board member/solicitor—view fundraising as empowering and ennobling rather than invasive and obnoxious, you will succeed. Fundraising techniques—which we discuss later—can be learned with relative ease. The real work is convincing you of the validity and decency of the fundraising enterprise.

EXERCISE 2B
Responding to a Solicitation

Participants: This exercise requires a facilitator and should be done with the entire board or the development committee.

The facilitator asks everyone to close his or her eyes, take three deep breaths, and imagine this scenario:

An old high school friend of yours has asked you to have lunch to discuss her work as a board member of a children's leukemia organization. She communicates her enthusiasm for the program and her deep respect for the staff and board members. She tells you a story about Maria, a lively seven-year-old who has leukemia. Two years ago, Maria had a chemotherapy treatment and lost all her hair; the leukemia appeared at the time to be in remission. Recently, however, Maria has undergone a bronchoscopy because her doctor fears a fungus has developed in her lungs. Her doctor now recommends a bone marrow transplant. He says the transplant will afford Maria a 75 percent chance of full recovery; without it, he gives her a year.

Your good friend now explains the role that you can play in helping the organization. Maria comes from a large family that has exhausted all its resources on her care. They need an additional $75,000 for the bone marrow operation. Your friend then asks for a contribution to help defray the costs for Maria's operation.

The facilitator then asks the group to open their eyes and think about how they would respond to the solicitation. The facilitator asks these questions and leads a discussion on each one:

- Do you fear that if you say no, your friendship will go down the drain?
- Are you embarrassed by your friend's request?
- Do you spend the entire time preparing to ask your friend for a big gift to your own organization?
- Do you agree to make a contribution? Why? Why not?

Time: Twenty to thirty minutes

People Love to Give Away Money

This may seem counterintuitive, but it's true: a warm and glowing feeling comes over people when they make big gifts. Our job as fundraisers is to give people the opportunity to feel good about themselves through the act of giving.

Nonprofit board members get in their own way all the time when it comes to fundraising because, as we have noted, they view the effort to solicit money as invasive, onerous, and embarrassing. The fact is, most people appreciate being asked, and they enjoy investing in a successful community enterprise.

EXERCISE 3

What Moves People to Give

Participants: This exercise requires a facilitator and should be done with the entire board.

The facilitator asks everyone to close his or her eyes, take three deep breaths, and consider this scenario:

> Imagine that you won $10 million in the lottery six months ago. Also assume you are someone who likes the limelight. Each year, your organization, of which you have been a board member for ten years, sponsors a large and festive sit-down dinner with many community members, public officials, and board members in attendance. Your organization has recently initiated a fundraising campaign to purchase a permanent facility and plans to announce the start of the campaign at this year's dinner.
>
> Having informed the organization that you would like to make a sizeable contribution to the building campaign, you have been asked to announce it at the dinner. You are dressed in your best suit or outfit for the evening and your family and friends are sharing your table. Music has been playing all evening and everyone is having a marvelous time. The music stops; the board chair comes to the podium. He or she reviews the fabulous work of your organization, explains the need for a permanent home, and announces the commencement of the campaign. You are called to the podium and are now standing at the dais about to hand the board chair a check for $500,000.

The facilitator then asks the group to open their eyes and think about these questions:

- What moves you about this moment?
- What brings tears to your eyes?
- Why have you chosen this organization?
- What would you say to honor the organization as you hand over the check?

The facilitator records the discussion points on a flipchart and initiates a discussion.

Time: Fifteen to twenty-five minutes

Consider even a partial list of the good things someone gets by making a financial contribution to a nonprofit organization:

- The satisfaction of helping an organization that is devoted to a cause about which the donor cares deeply

- The satisfaction of helping an organization that the donor knows is doing a great job

- The pleasure of responding positively to a friend or colleague who has made the solicitation

- The opportunity to invest in an enterprise that benefits the community

- The opportunity to be honored and celebrated for one's generosity

- The opportunity, through a memorial gift, to honor someone whom the donor loved

- The opportunity to create a legacy that will last long after the donor's passing

- The tax benefit (this is important in the realm of planned gifts but is of less consequence with regard to other types of contributions)

It bears restating: our job as fundraisers is to enable people to feel good about themselves. Our work isn't embarrassing; it's ennobling!

People Give Money to People

This is one of those hoary clichés in the world of fundraising that happens to be gospel truth. The most effective way to raise money is to make sure that the right solicitor asks the right prospect for a gift at the right dollar level at the right time. Like it or not, "who knows whom" is at least as important as what an organization is doing to benefit the world.

Those of you who haven't forgotten your high school geometry may remember the notion that something can be necessary but not sufficient. It is necessary for your organization to provide a valuable service in a cost-effective manner. It is necessary to write concise, hard-hitting letters of intent and full proposals. What gives fundraising sufficiency, however, is the right person asking the right other person for the gift.

Consider two scenarios in which your organization is attempting to get a grant from a foundation. In scenario A, your director of development writes an extraordinarily powerful funding proposal and sends it cold to the foundation (that is, your organization has no personal connection at the foundation).

In scenario B, the president of your board plays golf with the president of the foundation that is being solicited. No proposal has yet been submitted, but on the eighteenth green, the board president scribbles something about your organization and its needs on the back of an envelope and hands it to the foundation president. "Give this some thought, Darlene," says the board president. Which scenario is more likely to produce a grant? Scenario B, of course (provided that a well-written proposal follows upon this initial contact in a timely manner).

Here is a more modest but still pertinent example: a board member of a client of ours was approached recently by his next-door neighbor for a contribution to a nonprofit working to combat heart disease. There is no history of heart disease in this board member's family, but he gave his neighbor a contribution. Why? Because she asked for it. If she had approached him on behalf of an organization working to eradicate diabetes—there is no diabetes in his family either—would that have mattered one whit? No, he would have given her a contribution just as readily, simply because she asked for it! The personal connection, then, was paramount.

EXERCISE 4

The Personal Touch

Participants: This exercise requires a facilitator and should be done with the entire board.

The facilitator asks each person to read this text:

> It is near the holidays. You come home from a long day at work, take off your coat, and begin to look through the mail. Among the holiday cards, bills, and magazines are three letters. The first is from a national organization; above the printed return address on the outer envelope is the handwritten name of your dear college roommate whom you haven't seen in years. The second is from a neighbor down the street (the letter is a solicitation from a local nonprofit, but you can't tell that from the outer envelope). The third is from a local nonprofit (no personal identifier here).

Discuss:

- Which letters do you open?
- Which get put away for future consideration?
- Which go straight to the recycling bin?

Time: Ten to fifteen minutes

Your organization must therefore enlist all its board members, staff people, alums, volunteers, and other "organizational intimates" to solicit contributions from their friends, relatives, and colleagues. This constitutes your organization's initial hot list. Too many organizations focus their energy on strangers whom they believe will be interested in their work. Go after the folks you know first, and troll for interested strangers later.

Fundraising from the Perspective of the Donor, Not the Applicant

Fundraising is sales and marketing. That's right: sales and marketing. Raising funds is exactly like selling soap. If your friendly neighborhood multinational hand soap corporation wants to market a new brand of liquid soap, what does the company do? It convenes a focus group of potential consumers to ask them such questions as "What color should the soap be?" "How should the bottle be shaped?" "Is patchouli or vanilla a more desirable scent?"

Oddly enough, this is our job as fundraisers, too: to figure out what the customer—that is, the donor—wants, and to sell him or her our product without compromising our product's integrity. The single biggest mistake organizations make when they try to raise funds is that they trot out one and only one description of their work and cast that tasteless bread upon the funding waters.

An example: we served as fundraising counsel to a national public interest policy organization working on behalf of poor and mistreated children. We taught the board members these guidelines: if you are talking to someone of a politically conservative bent and you hope to raise big money, emphasize "combating juvenile delinquency." If you are talking instead to a liberal person, emphasize "empowering youth." The point was—and is—to talk the donor's talk without misrepresenting the organization.

Note here the importance of research. If we know the political predilections of our prospects, we can make the case much more effectively than if we're limited to guesswork. The more you know about a prospect, the more effective you'll be in your fundraising work. Board members are not expected to do formal research on prospective donors. All we want you to do is to give staff pertinent information about those friends and colleagues whom you intend to approach for contributions.

Consider the importance of research as it relates to securing a grant from a foundation. If your organization writes to twenty-five foundations, staff had better send twenty-five very different letters, each emphasizing the buzzwords of interest to the particular grantor. If the Endless Lucre Foundation uses the word *empowerment* fourteen times in its annual report, wouldn't it make sense to use the word *empowerment* in the letter you send to the Endless Lucre Foundation? This would seem obvious to the point of being simplistic, but most organizations don't get it. They write what they want about their organizations without giving any thought to what the customer/foundation wants to hear. Cookie-cutter letters simply will not fly.

Sales and marketing: we're selling concepts, not products, but we're salespeople and marketers nonetheless. That's why research is such an important part of fundraising. The more we know about a foundation—or corporation, or major donor, or recipient of a direct mail letter—the better we'll target the fundraising approach according to the interests of the particular prospect. Put yourself in your customer's shoes, and you'll be well on your way to raising big bucks.

EXERCISE 5
Organizational Sales Pitches

Participants: This exercise requires a facilitator and should be done with a small group composed of board members, other volunteers, and staff.

The facilitator asks everyone to discuss this scenario:

> Imagine that you will pursue three funders for your organization. What are three distinct ways in which you might describe the work of your organization so that it appeals to the specific interests of each funder, without misrepresenting the organization? For example, think about the pitch you might make to a politically conservative funder as opposed to a liberal one. Also consider emphasizing particular projects; for instance, if you have an after-school program and a reading program, which do you think would appeal to a donor whose child is dyslexic? Or perhaps you serve a minority population; what might you emphasize depending on the race or ethnicity of the donor? This is not about promoting stereotypes among donors but rather learning (and as we discuss later, researching) the particular proclivities of each potential funder.

Time: Twenty-five to thirty-five minutes

People Give to Strength, Not Crisis

There is a terrible temptation on the part of many organizations to throw themselves on the mercy of the donor: "Please, please, if you don't fund us, we'll go under in six months!" One can hardly imagine a more inept fundraising strategy.

Nobody cares that your nonprofit needs money. Every organization in the world needs more money than it has (and the huge majority of the *people* in the world need more money than they have as well). The fact that your organization needs money is of no consequence to anyone. On the other hand, the fact that your organization is doing good work and, with the donor's money, will do even better work as we move into the next year and the next decade—that's appealing.

Also, nobody in the philanthropic world appreciates a bargain. If you go to a foundation and say "we pay our executive director well below the market rate; think of the bang for the buck you're getting," what will the foundation representative think? Not "think of the bang for the buck we're getting," but "whom could they possibly get at a below-market rate?" Think big, believe in yourself, and you'll succeed at raising funds.

If you look at a donation to a nonprofit as an investment in a successful community enterprise, you'll understand the appropriateness of what we call "much has been done, much remains to be done" fundraising. Why would anyone invest in a sinking ship? It makes no sense. As a board member who is raising funds for your organization, your job is to alert prospective donors to the marvelous work of your organization and to educate them about the positive impact their contribution will have on your good work. You must always be upbeat; uncertainty or diffidence about your mission or programs spells fundraising disaster.

If your organization is just starting up—or if it's only a gleam in your mind's eye—your job is to excite prospective donors about the need for your new nonprofit and convince them that you have the expertise and experience to do a first-class job in meeting that need. Again, optimism and confidence will carry the day.

Fundraising is a confidence game in the finest sense of the term. Your job as a fundraising board member is to instill confidence in the mind of the donor that there is a need to be addressed and that your organization is the perfect vehicle to meet that need. You must also remain confident in your mission and your ability to raise money, no matter what the economic conditions. It is true that charitable giving fluctuates somewhat with economic ebbs and flows, but even in a persistent recession total giving is unlikely to dip more than a few percent.

We must add immediately that many organizations suffer from weaknesses that, if not addressed, hamper their fundraising. Did your accountant abscond last year with $50,000 and disappear into the Amazonian jungle? Did your administrative assistant unintentionally destroy all your donor records, making it impossible to thank everyone who gave to your last direct mail campaign? Did your organization get some bad press recently concerning the dust-up between your board chair and the executive director?

If there are skeletons in your organizational closet, it's time to confront them and develop responses to the criticisms that are likely to be voiced by prospective donors. "It's true," you might say, "that an unfortunate computer glitch kept us from generating thank-you letters to our generous direct mail donors last year. Fortunately, we have instituted a new system that catalogues donor information rapidly and comprehensively, and we anticipate no further difficulties." You should take donors' criticisms and concerns seriously, and you should demonstrate that you are taking steps to alleviate problems.

EXERCISE 6

Organizational Strengths and Weaknesses

Participants: This exercise requires a facilitator and should be done with the entire board. It is also advisable to have staff present to participate in the brainstorming session.

The facilitator for this exercise uses a flipchart and initiates the brainstorming. The focus of the brainstorming is on organizational and program strengths and weaknesses. Strengths might include the benefits your organization bestows on the community, staff and board expertise, and history of accomplishment. Weaknesses might include program goals that weren't met, populations that weren't served, or an embarrassing public dispute among board members.

Using the strengths to sell your organization, discuss how a donor investing in your successful enterprise might reap a return on his or her investment (a donor might invest in a possible cure for multiple sclerosis or cancer, or a job training program for individuals receiving government assistance, or sports and mentorship programs to reduce youth drug use).

With regard to weaknesses, has your organization had a problem that ended up in the press? If there is an issue that imperils your fundraising, you should discuss the steps that you plan to take in the next twelve to eighteen months to eliminate this problem. Brainstorm also about what keeps you from meeting all the needs you would like to address. For example, do you have sufficient staff to carry out your organization's mission?

Time: Thirty-five to forty-five minutes

Specificity Is Next to Godliness

Nothing inspires confidence like specificity. The impression you must leave with the donor is that you know how you will use the donor's money, who will benefit, what the outcomes will be, where the project will be located, and when the project will begin and end. All you need to ensure success is the donor's money; everything else is in place. Also, always be sure to use the future tense, not the conditional tense, in fundraising writing and speaking. Never say, "We would like to begin this project next June"; always say, "We will begin this project next June."

Specifics make the world of fundraising go 'round; vagueness kills fundraising. A lack of clarity about your target population, methodology, or any other aspect of your work leaves the prospective donor wondering, "Why should I invest in something so uncertain?"

As a board member, you should look to staff to give you specific information about every project that your organization currently offers and that it intends to offer in the next three years. Staff will do board members a great service by preparing a "cheat sheet" for them with answers to the most commonly asked questions about your nonprofit.

Vagueness has a cousin—another true undesirable—that we call the "trust-me attitude." Here bravado overwhelms specificity. Let's consider a program that provides services to physically disabled children and teenagers in a medium-sized city on the East Coast. The executive director thinks it would be a great idea to expand services to another population that is not currently being served in that city: emotionally disturbed teenagers.

The executive director visits an investment banker who is a prospective major donor. "As you know, Mike," the executive director says, "emotionally disturbed teenagers are a needy population that isn't getting a lot of help in our town. This is new territory for us, but our staff are smart and resourceful, and we understand teenagers. We can get the job done." In response, the prospect asks: "How big is this problem? Do you know how many emotionally disturbed teenagers live in our city? Do you have a project plan and budget? When do you intend to get started? Where?" The embarrassed executive director stammers that she will get back to him with the details.

Our savvy major donor prospect won't give the organization a penny. You must convince a person of three things when seeking his or her money: there is a need to be addressed, you represent the organization that will address that need, and you know specifically what you're going to do to address that need and how much it will cost. Our executive director has assumed that her organization's expertise with one population equips her program to offer services to another population—and she hasn't made the case.

What a difference if she says: "As you know, Mike, our needs assessment revealed that emotionally disturbed teenagers constitute 15 percent of the teenage population and aren't getting a lot of help in our town. We need to expand into this new area. Staff has been working on the proposed project plan and what it will cost; here are their findings for your review. I'm also excited that Lola Black, the former executive director of a residential program for emotionally disturbed teenagers, has agreed to head up our new program for this vulnerable population. Lola has twenty years of experience in this field, and if we can secure sufficient funding, we'll also be able to hire her former assistant." The executive director has now demonstrated the need and indicated why her program is appropriate to meet that need.

EXERCISE 7

Making the Case for Funding

Participants: This exercise requires a facilitator and should be done with a small group composed of development committee members, other volunteers, and staff.

The facilitator asks three individuals to volunteer to do a role play. The first role is a board member of your organization, the second is the executive director, and the third is a savvy program officer at a large local community foundation. Pick a project that your organization does not currently offer but that you feel would be a useful addition to your menu of services. Assume that a brief (and not too detailed) letter has been sent to the community foundation about the proposed project.

The foundation officer has invited you in to make the case for funding but has expressed some concern about this new project because it is outside your traditional program area. The board member's job is to make a pitch to the program officer for the new project. The executive director helps out when needed in making the case, and the program officer asks lots of detailed questions.

Everyone else should observe and take notes. After the group has finished, answer this list of questions:

- What aspects of the program did the board member and executive director describe well?
- What aspects were overlooked or given short shrift?
- What need will this program or service address?
- Which target population will benefit from the project?
- What will the geographical target area be?
- What are the desired objectives, goals, and measurable outcomes?
- What is the staffing for the project?
- What is the budget?
- Why is your organization the best qualified to provide this service or program?
- And the clincher question: How do you plan to provide resources for this program once the foundation's grant runs out?

Time: Forty-five to fifty-five minutes

Successful Fundraising Depends on Careful Record Keeping

As a board member, it is not your responsibility to log donations and keep donor information records. It is your responsibility to help your organization build a successful fundraising program, and this means ensuring that your organization has a systematic, functional record-keeping system.

A term that is used synonymously with fundraising is "cultivation." How can we cultivate a donor with an eye toward a larger gift in the future if we have little or no information about that person and his or her donor history?

Poor record keeping constitutes a nonprofit epidemic. Schools have no idea where their alums live; theater companies make no effort to keep former patrons in the fold; environmental organizations lose touch with their major donors. If you want to raise money successfully and consistently, you must make record keeping a top priority.

We cannot emphasize this too strongly: the best way to keep good records is to invest in good fundraising software. Here's a hypothetical story to demonstrate the importance of good software. In the spring of this year, Susan Vibrato, a board member of the Diva Fever Music Society, successfully solicits a gift of $1,000 from Jane Bux, a good friend of Susan's. The principal reason that Jane makes the gift is that her friend Susan has asked for it.

Six months later, Susan Vibrato leaves the board of the Diva Fever Music Society and moves across country. When the society is ready to pursue a second gift from Jane Bux next spring, who will make the approach? Not Susan Vibrato—she's no longer on the scene. What does the society know about Jane Bux? Absolutely nothing, because Susan kept all her information about Jane to herself, including the particulars of the conversation that Susan and Jane had when Susan first approached Jane for a major gift. Does the Music Society even know if a thank-you note was sent?

If the Diva Fever Music Society had simply invested in fundraising software—which need not be expensive—they would have had the ability to call up, with the stroke of a key, this information:

- Jane Bux's address, phone, and e-mail

- The amount that she gave to the society in the past

- The date on which she made her gift

- A brief description of the conversation that Susan had with Jane, including the aspects of the Diva Fever Music Society's activities that were of greatest interest to Jane

- Biographical information (from Susan or a staff person who conducted Internet research on Jane)

Investing in good fundraising software means purchasing and learning how to use a good fundraising database system, not one created by a volunteer who quits shortly after all the data has been entered, leaving no instructions and inaccessible data. There are numerous fundraising applications available, from free programs at nonprofit support centers to powerful database programs tailored specifically for your organization costing in excess of $10,000.

A basic program enables you to perform simple operations such as indexing, sorting, and mail merging. A fancier program enables you to generate a wider variety of reports, customized letters, e-mails, thank-you

---

EXERCISE 8

Donor Record Keeping

Participants: This exercise requires a facilitator and should be done in a confidential manner with a small group of development committee members and staff.

Prior to conducting the exercise, the facilitator asks staff to select a large donor to your organization and produce a full report on this person, using only current written and database records. With this information in hand, how many of these questions can you answer? (What we are doing is assessing the quality of your donor records.)

- What is the donor's connection to the organization?
- What was the dollar size of the donor's initial gift?
- What was the gift's purpose?
- What was the dollar size of the donor's most recent gift? What was its purpose?
- What is the donor's profession or business?
- What else do you know about the donor's financial situation?
- To which social circle does the donor belong?
- To which other organizations has the donor contributed?
- What aspects of your organization are of particular interest to the donor?
- Do you know the donor's date of birth?
- What do you know about the donor's family?
- Who has access to this information?

Note: Confidentiality is of the utmost importance to ensure donor privacy. All information will to the maximum extent possible be kept within the room. We recommend also that your organization purchase a database security system so that only a limited number of people can gain access to information about donors and prospects. Those who would have access might include the executive director and the volunteers responsible for soliciting gifts.

Time: Twenty-five to thirty-five minutes

notes, and other material. A program tailored for a large organization can manage large databases and be accessed from multiple sites. Some research and a thoughtful assessment of your organization's needs and budget will help steer you toward the right package. Staff will be responsible for locating and purchasing the best software, but the board must make sure that fundraising software is a priority and approve an appropriate amount of money for acquisition and training staff in its use.

Ten Percent of the People Give 90 Percent of the Money

Many organizations do a bang-up job of getting that first, modest contribution from a donor via direct mail, telephone solicitation, or sale of a ticket to a small special event. That's well and good, but most of these nonprofits never ratchet up; they continue to ask their donors for small contributions when a significant number of them could give a great deal more if asked appropriately. Most of the money donated to nonprofits comes from the relatively small number of folks who have the wherewithal to make big gifts. According to Boston College's Social Welfare Research Institute, families with incomes over $500,000—they constitute 1 percent of the population—make 26 percent of all charitable contributions in the United States.[3] It is vitally important that your organization be ready to pursue the folks who can help the most.

As a board member who is part of your organization's fundraising team, it is your job to provide information concerning how much someone might give, and ask that person for the appropriate amount. Every day of the week organizations are sending direct mail letters to donors who could give more money if asked appropriately. As fundraising consultants, this breaks our heart. Please understand that we do not wish to diminish the importance of the $50 direct mail or telephone contributor: salt of the earth when it comes to fundraising, and today's modest contributor is tomorrow's major donor. But if someone can give your organization $50,000 now, isn't he or she worth at least as much of your time and effort as the person who can give $50?

The most effective way on earth to raise money is to sit across the table from someone who has lots of it and ask for some. Think about it: a direct mail letter gives you no clue concerning the prospective donor's reaction to your appeal. A telephone solicitation affords only oral cues. A face-to-face solicitation yields both oral and visual cues and is therefore the most effective kind to ask.

As a fundraiser of our acquaintance is fond of saying in contrasting direct mail with major gift solicitation, "If you want to get milk from a cow, you don't send the cow a letter; you have to go to the source and squeeze!"

EXERCISE 9

Who Are Your Major Donors?

Participants: This exercise requires a facilitator and should be done confidentially with a small group of development committee members and staff.

This exercise is a great start in figuring out who your major donors might be. Prior to conducting the exercise, the facilitator asks staff to give the development committee a comprehensive list of all individual donations made in the past two years. (Do not include grants, only individual donations.) The development committee should consider:

- What was the average gift (total dollars raised divided by the number of donors)?
- How many donors gave above the average?
- Who constituted the top 10 percent of donors?
- If you took away the top 10 percent, how much money would remain?
- Did most of your contributions come from just a few donors, thus skewing the average?

Time: Fifteen to twenty-five minutes

Donors' Gifts Must Be Recognized Imaginatively

Your organization's best source of revenue is folks who have already donated to your organization. This is no mystery; people who have shown an interest in your nonprofit through past contributions should—if cultivated intelligently and consistently—continue to give.

Sadly, some organizations make the unfortunate error of accepting that first contribution and disappearing into the sunset—sometimes without even saying "thank you"—never to be heard from again. This is impolite, and it's bad fundraising. The thank-you letter that you send upon receipt of a donor's first gift is the first step in securing a second gift.

As a board member, you never want your organization to get a call asking: "I sent you a check six weeks ago. Didn't you get it?" Your role is to encourage staff to create and maintain a system to ensure that every donor is thanked within five working days of receiving the gift.

As indicated earlier, keep in mind also the critical importance of cultivation. With e-mail and the Web, it is easier than ever before to keep your donors apprised of your activities via e-newsletters and website updates, as well as through more traditional means such as print newsletters and informational mailings. Such cultivation activities are usually the staff's responsibility, but it's a good idea for board members to volunteer occasionally to write newsletter columns or e-mail updates.

Thank-you letters, newsletters, and the like are an important start in cultivating donors. But the effort can't stop there, especially when it comes to thanking your most important donors. You must recognize your donors promptly and imaginatively. What is your organization doing to recognize donors? Listing them in your newsletter? Mounting a plaque with their names on your reception area wall? Hosting a party for major donors? Whatever you're doing, you can probably do more.

One reason that people make contributions to nonprofit organizations is that they are recognized and honored for their gifts. There is nothing patronizing, obsequious, or corny about celebrating donors' gifts. Think of it as a *quid pro quo*: the donor makes a contribution, and you thank and honor the donor in return. Organizations that truly "get" donor recognition send birthday cards to major donors and telegrams of congratulation when major donors' children graduate from college. Here are some other recognition ideas:

- An event designed specifically to honor donors, not to ask for money.

- A naming opportunity. Although capital campaigns present the most obvious context for a naming opportunity, it is applicable in more modest campaigns as well. How about placing the name of a donor on a classroom computer or a piece of medical equipment?

- A press release with donors' names displayed prominently.

- A book or report issued by the nonprofit that includes acknowledgment of donors.

Here's a helpful hint for the board: new board members with no experience in fundraising can get their feet wet in their first year of board service by calling major donors simply to thank them for their gifts. The new board member is not yet asking for money, but he or she is participating in a vitally important aspect of cultivation and is communicating directly with donors.

When we conduct fundraising trainings, we are occasionally asked, "What about donors who request anonymity? Shouldn't we simply leave them alone?" Our response is: if a donor requests anonymity, you certainly should honor that request. If a donor does not request anonymity, however, he or she does not wish to be anonymous! People love to be celebrated, stroked, and revered for their contributions. Organizations must honor donors.

EXERCISE 10

Donor Recognition

Participants: This exercise requires a facilitator and should be done with the entire board, the executive director, and the director of development.

The facilitator records findings on a flipchart. Make a list of the ways in which your organization currently recognizes donors. Next, brainstorm new donor recognition activities that your nonprofit might consider in the future.

Create two lists. The first, for large donors, might include items such as:

- A meeting featuring well-known speakers
- A tour of the facilities led by program staff
- A donor recognition party
- A seminar on issues related to the organization's work

Items for smaller donors might include:

- Goodie bags at a special event
- Token trinkets with the name of the organization, such as pens, cups, calendars, calculators, pocket-knives, and so on
- Items specific to the nonprofit's field of endeavor (for instance, seeds or small plants for an environmental organization)

Let your imagination go; be creative. Once you've listed all suggestions, give this list to the development committee to review, and choose a few you can do in the next year.

Time: Twenty-five to thirty-five minutes

Good Fundraising Is Opportunistic

It's an unfortunate fact, but fundraising is trendy. If your organization's issue is on the front page, it's easy to raise money. If your issue is not on the front page, it's tougher.

An obvious implication: get on the front page. All nonprofits understand that they have to raise money; too few understand that public relations and media relations are every bit as important as fundraising. Indeed, fundraising is virtually impossible without good public relations. The best-kept secret doesn't raise money.

Fundraising is simply opportunism on behalf of a good cause. If your issue is getting serious public exposure, make the effort to raise money as soon as is feasible. Be opportunistic!

Let us give a horrific but pertinent example from our files. A few years ago, a woman in a western state who operated a board and care facility for seniors was accused—and eventually convicted—of murdering some of her residents and burying them in the backyard. The story was headline news throughout the state.

Our client—which worked exclusively on behalf of seniors—was at the time heavily involved in the issue of proper licensing of board and care facilities. The organization had submitted a number of proposals to foundations to fund this work but had heard nothing. The press coverage of the

---

EXERCISE 11

Securing Press Coverage

Participants: This exercise requires a facilitator and should be done with all board members.

The facilitator uses a flipchart and begins by having participants brainstorm the major events or trends of the past year that are related to the work of your organization. For example:

- A foster child dies in a nearby county (you run a group home for youths).
- A tornado strikes your town and ruins a major housing project where many of your clients live.
- A study is released demonstrating that youths who have mentors have a better chance of future success than those who do not; you run a big brother or big sister program.

Then add to the list pertinent current events on a flipchart.

After you have created the list, brainstorm how your organization might take advantage of coverage in the electronic and print media. Here are some ideas to get you started:

- Include quotes from the press in a direct mail letter.
- Have a small special event with a speaker who was in the news in your subject area.
- Ask someone who was in the news on a related issue to join your board.
- Issue a press release on a current event that relates to your work.

Also brainstorm a protocol for responding when these opportunities present themselves. Who is responsible for keeping an eye on these opportunities? What will your organization do if an opportunity for increased public exposure presents itself?

Time: Twenty-five to thirty-five minutes

murders led several foundations to contact the program and, once one foundation funded the project, others jumped on board. Before the organization knew it, they were given more money than they had asked for to tackle the board and care licensing issue. Without the press coverage, it is highly doubtful that the project would have secured sufficient funding.

Fundraising is an emotional, not a logical, business. When people are particularly sensitive to the importance of your issue and your work, you must make the effort to raise funds. Find reporters in the print and electronic media who are interested in your issue, and whom you can educate about your organization. The higher the profile you have in the community, the easier it is to raise funds.

Notes

1. California Youth Connection mission statement, a statewide nonprofit in California, http://www.calyouthconn.org/

2. *Giving USA,* a publication of the AAFRC Trust for Philanthropy, researched and written by the Center on Philanthropy at Indiana University.

   http://aafrc.org/

3. Based on data from the "Survey of Consumer Finances 2001" and calculated by researchers at the Boston College Social Welfare Research Institute.

   http://www.bc.edu/research/swri/

Chapter 3

The Board's Role in Specific Fundraising Activities

ZIMMERMAN LEHMAN has never had a client—no matter how sophisticated about fundraising, no matter how many resources the client was pouring into development—that was raising funds in every appropriate way. Be it corporate solicitation, planned giving, direct mail, major gift approaches, or any of a host of other strategies, every organization in our experience has missed at least one bet. We are therefore intent on ensuring that your nonprofit diversifies its fundraising effort and makes appropriate use of your board of directors in every area.

In this chapter, we familiarize you with the techniques to guarantee your ability to raise the funds necessary for your nonprofit's survival and growth. This chapter is intended to educate you, the board member, about fundraising strategies and your role in planning and implementing each technique. These techniques create the opportunity for individuals or grantors to invest in your worthy community enterprise.

Above all, you must understand that the savvy nonprofit organization diversifies its funding base. Why is it so important to diversify? Let's take the example of two national public policy youth organizations. For many years, organization A was funded almost entirely by federal grants. Organization B, on the other hand, hired a development director who prepared a fundraising plan and raised money from a variety of sources (individuals, foundations, corporations, and government agencies). When a new administration in Washington cut federal funding for public policy work dramatically, who do you think carried on more effectively? Organization B simply continued doing what it was doing and was not seriously hampered by the reduction in government funding. The name of the game, then, is to diversify your development effort (just as your financial adviser would tell you to diversify your personal investments).

We have grouped nonprofit fundraising techniques in three sections: individual contributions, contributions from businesses, and grants.

Individual Contributions

Solicitation of gifts from individuals is of the utmost importance to every nonprofit organization intent on doing effective fundraising, and the board's role is key. In this section we present the various ways that an organization approaches individuals for a contribution. As you will see, consistent and imaginative use of the board of directors is vitally important to the success of each approach.

Although it is certainly important to pursue grants from institutional sources (foundations, businesses, religious philanthropies, and government agencies), you must understand that, in the world of philanthropy, grants are considered "soft money." That is, grants are almost always time-limited and are subject to political winds and the idiosyncrasies of grantor board members.

On the other hand, an individual donor who believes in your cause and who has been properly cultivated will see your organization through thick and thin. There are three reasons individual solicitation should be the focus of your organization's development effort.

Individuals Make 80–90 Percent of All Private Gifts

Year after year, the American Association of Fundraising Counsel's statistics on private giving to charities in the United States (that is, gifts from individuals, foundations, corporations, and religious philanthropies, but not government agencies) reveal that between 80 and 90 percent of these gifts—amounting to hundreds of billions of dollars annually—come from individuals.[1] Any organization that thinks it can float on grants is tragically mistaken; the huge majority of private philanthropic contributions come from individuals.

Most Individual Gifts Constitute Unrestricted Income

If your organization conducts a mail campaign, asks for gifts by phone, or sells tickets to a special event, the income derived from these efforts can be used in any fashion you deem appropriate (as opposed, say, to a grant from a foundation, which is usually given for a specific project). The nicest money to raise, obviously, is unrestricted money. Nonprofits often, for example, have difficulty finding funds to hire development staff. A sufficient pool of unrestricted funds enables an organization to hire competent fundraisers.

Gifts from Individuals Can Increase Dramatically over Time

If an individual gives your organization a contribution, and if you cultivate that person with intelligence, respect, and imagination, there is every reason to expect more and larger gifts from that person into the future. This potential rarely exists with grants.

The organization that understands fundraising realizes that effective individual solicitation depends upon creating a system. Successful solicitation of a contribution via a mail campaign opens the way for inviting the donor to a special event, and his or her enjoyment of the special event opens the way for a major or planned gift in the future. No effort to raise funds from individuals should be viewed in isolation; a successful system of individual solicitation includes the means to keep records about how much someone has given, in what context he or she made the gift (event, mail appeal), and what motivated him or her to give.

Let's look at this a bit more closely. If your organization hosts a cocktail party fundraiser, invests one thousand person-hours in the event, and nets only $10,000, why, you might ask yourself, did we bother with the event at all? The answer is: you didn't do it for the $10,000; you did it for the ninety-eight new donors who attended the event and whom you will solicit again and again in the coming months and years. Your modest event, then, may well constitute the first step in raising many millions. Fundraising is not a quick-fix business. Do not be seduced into spending all your fundraising time writing grant proposals that appear to offer more immediate bang for

EXERCISE 12

Why Would Someone Make a Gift to Your Organization? (or: Why Would Someone Not Make a Gift?)

Participants: This exercise requires a facilitator and should be done with the entire board, especially if the board has not previously done much solicitation of individuals. Staff can also participate in this exercise or do the same exercise at a staff meeting.

The facilitator records the proceedings on a flipchart, asking participants to brainstorm the reasons that someone might make a large donation to your organization. He or she then asks them to brainstorm why someone might not make a large donation.

Discuss these concerns and criticisms, and come up with "party-line" responses. You are now beginning to create the "case" for why an individual should make a donation to your organization.

Time: Twenty-five to thirty-five minutes

the buck than an individual campaign. Pursuing grants is important, but board members must insist on building a system of individual solicitation that ultimately generates significant income.

Let us now examine in detail the techniques that nonprofits employ to solicit contributions from individuals:

- Direct mail

- Special events

- Telephone solicitation

- Major donor solicitation

- Planned gift solicitation

- Website and e-mail requests

Direct Mail

Many nonprofit board and staff members hold direct mail in low esteem. Everyone is inundated with appeal letters every day; they reason, why should anyone bother with our letter? In fact, a carefully targeted direct mail campaign is a highly effective means for unearthing new donors and getting larger gifts from current donors. Board members play a critical role in ensuring the success of a direct mail campaign by sending letters to your friends and colleagues that include a personal note alerting your "intimates" to the importance of the organization.

To enlist board members' support for the direct mail effort, it is important that you understand how a direct mail campaign is planned and built. A successful campaign depends on:

- Lists of solid prospects (potential donors) who might be interested in making an initial gift or a larger gift

- An effective letter, return device, and other enclosures

- Dependable "mailing mechanics" (printing, stuffing, sealing, and mailing)

- Appending a personal note

Prospect Lists

Fundraising is a series of widening concentric circles. The innermost circle comprises board members, volunteers, alums, and clients. The next circle is made up of friends, relatives, and colleagues of folks in the innermost circle. Board members and others in the innermost circle must prepare lists of friends and colleagues who might make a modest contribution via direct mail. This is very important, but board members should also realize that the inner circle hot list is never sufficient to fuel a serious direct mail effort.

Organizations that take full advantage of direct mail turn to knowledgeable list brokers, who supply them with names and addresses of likely donors and do trial runs to see which package gets the best returns. The Internet revolution has been a boon for researchers who chart people's philanthropic interests, political persuasions, and newspaper and periodical preferences. Once a list broker knows what an organization does and where it operates, the broker can prepare lists of likely donors based on hard research data. The direct mail campaign is therefore aimed at both the inner circle hot list and strangers who might be convinced to give.

Nonprofits should also consider trading lists with other organizations. We recommend bartering between organizations that have similar views but are not working in the same subject area. A community health clinic, for example, might want to trade with a local housing advocacy organization.

The Mailer

The mailer is a letter (usually two or three pages, though campaigns using twelve-page letters have been successful) describing the wonderful work of the organization and plans for the future, and asking for a gift. Also included is a return device on which donors indicate the amount they are giving and whether they would like to pledge a gift over a two- or three-year period. Some mailers include an additional promotional piece (perhaps a copy of a newspaper article extolling the virtues of the organization or a small token gift such as a pin or sticker).

Preparation of the direct mail letter, return device, and other enclosures is a staff, not board, responsibility. The board (specifically, the fundraising committee) can be useful in making overall recommendations for the campaign (for example, suggesting that the direct mail piece have a photograph or slogan that connects the outer envelope to the letter and all other enclosures). The staff should propose a theme for the campaign; it is the board's responsibility to approve that theme or to ask staff to go back to the drawing board.

Mechanics

In addition to preparing the letter, staff is responsible for the mechanics of stamping, stuffing, and sorting. Staff can either arrange a volunteer party to address these tasks or hire a mailing house. We heartily recommend the latter course except for very small campaigns. Mailing houses are affordable and take the worry and tedium out of "making the drop."

Personal Notes

Once the letter is ready, board members must append personal notes to the letters that their contacts will receive. There is nothing corny or pushy about such an exercise. Remember: the most important reason that anyone makes an initial contribution to an organization is that the right person asks for the gift.

The chief tactical issue in direct mail is persuading the recipient to open the envelope. We therefore counsel board members to do this: when sending a letter to a friend of yours on behalf of your organization, make sure to write your name at the top left-hand corner of the outer envelope above the name and address of the nonprofit. Your friend gets the letter, knows nothing about the organization, but says to himself: "I wonder why Cheryl is involved with this organization." To satisfy his curiosity, he opens the envelope. Voilà! We have solved the biggest direct mail problem.

The note that you append to the direct mail letter to a friend need not be long; it must be heartfelt. Here are some examples:

> *You're aware, Ramon, that I've been on the board of the Homeless Prenatal Program for the last five years. The work they do on behalf of homeless women and families simply astounds me. . . . I hope you can help out.[2]*

> *Taeko, the Homeless Prenatal Program has led the way in protecting the health and safeguarding the rights of homeless women and families. Your gift would make a big difference, and I'd really appreciate it.*

> *Did you know, Tanya, that hundreds of families sleep in shelters or on the street in our city every night? Your contribution will go a long way in helping the Homeless Prenatal Program to improve the lives of those who need us most.*

Four weeks after the drop (that is, after the letters have been sent), board members have an important follow-up role to play. Let us assume that each board member has sent letters to ten friends. If four of those friends have responded with gifts in the four weeks following the drop and six have not, the board member should pick up the phone and call the six friends who have yet to donate. A friendly phone call may well move the letter from the bottom of the friend's pile to the top.

EXERCISE 13

Direct Mail—Personal Notes

Participants: This exercise requires a facilitator and should be done with the entire board.

The facilitator asks participants to prepare several variations of personal notes they might append to a direct mail letter from your organization. (See the chapter text for three suggestions to get you started.) Write each of them on the flipchart and save them for use when you're ready to send the letters.

Time: Ten to twenty minutes

Special Events

In our experience, no fundraising approach is as consistently misunderstood as the special event. Organizations with little experience in planning and implementing events assume that the right event will net them an enormous amount of revenue (and that the more events, the better).

The reason many organizations struggle with events is that they haven't asked themselves a basic question: What do we want our event to accomplish? That is, do we want to make as much money as possible (in which case, a black-tie dinner and silent auction in a big downtown hotel might be just the thing)? Or do we want to alert the local community to who we are and what we do (in which case a low-cost tour of your facilities would be appropriate)?

Once the board has determined what you want the event to accomplish, you have a better sense of the kind of event that is appropriate. Here's a small sampling of types you might consider: luncheon, dinner, silent auction, live auction, film or theater benefit, day at the races, day at the ballpark, casino night, 10K race, walkathon, danceathon, bikeathon, or open house.

Events are labor-intensive, exhausting, and often chock full of peril. Whatever can go wrong very well might. Horror stories abound. Our firm ran an event in the sumptuous ballroom of a downtown hotel in a large city on the West Coast some years back. The ballroom was famous for its gorgeous glass ceiling. On the night of the event, a sudden storm pelted the area with intense rain. The glass ceiling was not equal to the rainstorm, and raindrops made their way between the glass panels. That's right: white-tied and begowned attendees enjoyed the pitter-pat of raindrops on their well-coiffed heads and dinner plates.

Why Hold an Event?

We are big fans of events for three reasons. First, and most important, a popular event enables your organization to capture new donors. A person who knows nothing about your organization or the subject area in which you work may well attend your event because he or she:

- Can't wait to hear that extraordinary speaker
- Was told that the chef prepares heavenly crayfish étouffée
- Loves the honoree
- Can't figure out any other way to see the inside of Mr. and Ms. Dinero's mansion atop the hill

Once that person shows up at the event, you have the opportunity to educate him or her about your organization with written material, a speech by your board president, and informal chats with other board members strategically positioned around the room. Also, it is vitally important to get the name, address, phone number, and e-mail address of every attendee (a sign-up at the registration desk is useful in this regard, as is a raffle). Now that the attendee has been "captured," you can approach him or her in the future to make direct mail contributions, to buy tickets to other special events, and perhaps down the line to become a major donor.

We'll never forget talking with a new client who was very proud of a recent outdoor benefit concert that had featured a famous rock band and netted the organization more than $50,000. "That's great," we said to the client. "And you did get the name, address, and e-mail address of everyone who bought a ticket, right?" The client looked at us blankly. What a fundraising tragedy: the $50,000 raised at the event was inconsequential compared to the money that might have been raised over many years had the organization captured information about the event attendees.

The second reason to hold an event is to give your organization a higher public profile. There is nothing like a dinner featuring a famous emcee, spellbinding speaker, and much-loved honoree to garner press and public acclaim. Remember: best-kept secrets don't raise money. If your organization is to be successful in the fundraising game, you must be known to the person on the street. When choosing the kind of event that your organization will host, be sure to consider the potential to secure significant press coverage. Some events (say, a day at the ballpark) are not so labor-intensive but don't have much ability to secure that higher profile. Others (for instance, a sit-down dinner with a live auction) have great profile potential but are terribly labor-intensive.

The final reason that an event makes sense for your organization is that it can—in some instances—raise significant money. We know of events that have netted $1 million and more; it can be done. Although your organization may be miles away from generating that kind of money the first time it hosts an event, by the tenth time you should have gained the traction to bring in big bucks. When an organization holds a top-quality event annually, it secures a place on your community's social calendar. Whether you are hosting an event for the first time or the twentieth, there are many ways to boost event income, among them corporate sponsorship, a raffle, an auction, and offering several price levels to ticket purchasers (an "individual sponsor" seat costs $350 or more and includes mention in the program; a regular seat costs $250 and does not include such mention). Don't view events as a fundraising panacea, but make sure to take advantage of every fundraising opportunity that an event offers.

The significance of board involvement in an event cannot be overstated. Events should not be managed by staff. Instead, in this context *staff* should be viewed as a verb: they staff the volunteer committee that oversees the event. The event committee is composed of board fundraising committee members and other volunteers who have a flair for organizing events that are entertaining and compelling, and who have contacts with individuals and businesses that will provide partial event underwriting. The committee is responsible for every major decision pertaining to the event, from date and locale to ticket prices and program.

Case Study: A Sit-down Dinner

How do staff and committee members work together effectively? Let us use a sit-down dinner as an example. The committee for such an event should meet at least six times. If you have nine months between the first meeting and the event, we suggest meeting every month for the first three months, and every other month for the final six months, with the understanding that an emergency meeting might need to be convened at any time should circumstances warrant.

At its first meeting, the dinner committee decides upon the dollar goal for the event. Decisions must then be made (at this meeting and the next) concerning event locale, date, ticket prices (both sponsorships and individual tickets), food and drink, emcee, speaker, and honoree. Committee members must also decide how many individual tickets each member is asked to sell, and who else (staff, ex-board members, other volunteers) is expected to peddle tickets.

By the third meeting, the committee should have made all decisions concerning the site, speaker, and honoree (you need not have both a speaker and an honoree, but the combination can help to sell tickets). The committee must also decide how to publicize the event; it is the staff's responsibility to implement the committee's recommendations about publicity. Again, however, if a committee member has an in with a local reporter, it is that member's responsibility to make the connection.

If the committee decides to hold a fancy dress dinner, dance, and silent auction at a downtown hotel, the committee asks the staff (usually the director of development) to visit three or four hotels to examine the banquet facilities and secure information on menu options and prices. The staff member obtains exhaustive information on the hotels, and the committee then decides which hotel to honor with its business. Staff is responsible for making formal arrangements with the hotel or other site and taking care of all program arrangements (scheduling the speaker, purchasing the wine, getting the names of the honoree's family in order to send them complimentary invitations, and so on). Committee members should make every effort to secure underwriting for the event and to convince the hotel to offer a nonprofit discount.

Committee members must understand the crucial role they play in selling tickets. Let's use a dinner benefiting an environmental organization as an example. Assume that individual tickets cost $200, a "sponsored" table of ten is $2,000, and the environmental nonprofit hopes to persuade fifteen energy companies and other major corporations in town to be sponsors. It would be pointless to ask the environmental organization's development

---

EXERCISE 14

Evaluating and Planning Your Special Event

Participants: This exercise requires a facilitator and should be done with the special events committee, the executive director, and development staff. The exercise is particularly helpful as part of the evaluation of your special event or in preparation for the next event.

Prior to the meeting, the facilitator asks development staff to prepare a short written summary of the event that was held. The group discusses whether your event was more successful in attracting community members or in raising money. If there is no clear answer, ask the group to decide which they would have preferred and why. Then brainstorm how your next event can succeed in meeting your chosen event goal. If your organization has never held an event, use these questions as the means for planning your first event.

If attracting more members is the issue, discuss these matters:

- Did you charge too much and therefore not have sufficient attendance?
- Did you publicize the event effectively?
- Was there a speaker who might have attracted more attendees?

If on the other hand you did not make enough money, you might ask:

- Did you charge too little?
- Were your expenses too high?
- Did you have enough sponsors? Any sponsors?
- Did every board member help solicit sponsorships or sell tickets?
- Was the event too complex and labor-intensive given the volunteers and resources at your disposal?

Also discuss whether your organization captured every attendee's address, phone number, and e-mail address. If not, decide how you will do this at your next event. (Consider a raffle, a sign-up card on the table, or a guest sign-in book.)

Time: Forty-five to sixty minutes

staff person to call the companies to sell sponsorships. Instead, committee members should decide who has the best contact at each company, and it should be the appropriate member's responsibility to call his or her contact to sell the sponsorship. Remember: fundraising is a peer-to-peer business.

Finally, don't forget to thank your attendees. Thank-you notes are a staff responsibility, but the committee should make sure they are sent out promptly.

Telephone Solicitation

Many organizations turn their noses up at telephone solicitation, for obvious reasons: you sit down to a tasty dinner at 7:00 P.M. on a Thursday evening only to be interrupted by someone who wants a contribution. Trouble is, the solicitor knows next to nothing about the nonprofit for which he or she is soliciting funds, and the solicitation has all the charm of a dead rat.

The problem is not that telephone solicitation is done; rather, it's done badly! Consider instead this scenario: your local humane society trains its board members in the art and science of telephone solicitation and puts together a list of past donors and others interested in animals. The volunteers make their calls courteously and informatively and at an appropriate time of day. ("How's your dog Stella? Thanks so much for your gift last fall, and we'd love to tell you about our new project on behalf of homeless dogs.") Is this invasive or obnoxious? Certainly not. Will it be successful? Definitely.

Telephone solicitation works so long as the calls are made by individuals who have an emotional investment in the organization, and so long as the callers are trained to make the approach properly. Here again, the board is vitally important. If a private elementary school wants to raise money from parents, grandparents, and alums, the school should establish a phone bank (a board member who works in a real estate office—where there are lots of telephones—might donate the use of his or her professional space). The phones should be staffed by board members and other volunteers who care about the school and who have been trained to make the pitch.

A final note here: there are certainly reputable telephone solicitation firms that have done excellent work on behalf of nonprofits. A useful rule of thumb is to look for firms that charge a flat fee, not a percentage of what they raise. For unscrupulous operators, percentage-based fundraising offers the opportunity to prey on people's honorable charitable instincts and to keep most of the money themselves.

EXERCISE 15

Telephone Follow-up to a Direct Mail Appeal

Participants: This exercise requires a facilitator and should be done with the development committee.

The facilitator divides the group into pairs for a role play. One person plays a board member who, one month ago, sent a direct mail letter with a personal note to a friend. The board member is now calling his or her friend—the other person in the role play—to move the letter to the top of the pile. The board member must ascertain that the letter was received and must find out if the friend has any questions about the organization or the direct mail campaign. Make the effort to nail down a contribution during the call.

After the role play, answer these questions:

- Could you answer your friend's questions?
- Did your friend seem offended by your pitch? If so, what did you do to make him or her more comfortable?
- What could you have done differently?
- Did the friend make a contribution or ask for more information?

Then switch roles and do the role play again.

Time: Thirty-five to forty-five minutes

Major Donors

The greatest gap between potential and reality in nonprofit fundraising is in the area of major donor solicitation. Every day organizations are sending letters to folks who could make contributions of $50,000 or $500,000 but are only being asked for $50. Every organization should be thankful for small contributions from donors of modest means, but it is wise to keep in mind, as we noted in Chapter Two, that 90 percent of donations to nonprofits come from 10 percent of the donors. It is no exaggeration to state that the principal reason to do any sort of individual donor appeal is to locate the relatively small number of contributors who have the ability to make a large gift. The individual who contributed $250 to your direct mail campaign, or who purchased six tickets to your fundraising dinner, probably has the interest and the wherewithal to make a significantly larger contribution.

Many organizations do an excellent job of prospecting for modest individual donations through direct mail, phone solicitation, and special events. What they fail to do is to review their donors with an eye toward pursuing those individuals who might make major gifts. Organizations that are serious about increasing their revenues must determine which of their friends and colleagues have the ability to make big gifts. It is then the job of the major donor committee to solicit these gifts in an organized and timely manner. In no fundraising area will the board have a greater positive impact than in major giving.

What Constitutes a Major Donor?

The category of "major donor" does not imply any particular dollar amount. A major donor to a prestigious private hospital is at a dollar level considerably higher than a major donor to a fledgling dance company. The major donor contribution is always substantially larger than the average individual gift to the nonprofit and is always solicited face-to-face, not by mail, phone, or e-mail. For some organizations, $500 is considered a major gift; for others it may be $500,000. Why face-to-face? Because the most effective way in the whole world to raise money is to sit across the table from someone who has a great deal of it and ask for some. The in-person solicitation affords the askers invaluable oral and visual cues that, as we shall see, aid them in pursuit of the gift. Ultimately, as we said earlier, fundraising is an emotional business, not a logical one, and talking to a prospect face-to-face offers the best possibility of moving him or her emotionally.

As a board member, you are particularly well positioned to ensure the success of your organization's major donor campaign. You are probably familiar with many of the current donors to your institution who have the ability to make a larger gift if asked appropriately, and you may have other friends or colleagues in mind who have this capability.

How Do You Find Major Donors?

The board plays a vital role in identifying potential big givers. Begin with your own donor base and review the gifts made to your organization by your largest contributors. These are the individuals who constitute the inner circle of your major donor prospect pool. If your program has never solicited individual contributions, you probably need to backtrack a step and begin with a direct mail or telephone campaign. It is the rare organization that can jump into major donor solicitation without having raised smaller individual contributions first.

Review your membership lists, read the society pages to find out who has made large gifts recently to organizations like yours, and most important brainstorm with other board members and staff about individuals they know who have the ability to make major gifts and who are interested in the work of your organization (or could become interested with appropriate persuasion). Pay particular attention to past members of your board of directors, as well as to friends and colleagues of board and staff. Remember: even a small organization has major donor potential.

The Importance of Research

We should mention too that research is critical to cultivating and soliciting a prospect. The more you know about your prospect, the easier it is to make the case for a major donation successfully. Board members should conduct confidential anecdotal research by reviewing the list of prospects and providing information about the prospects whom they know personally. This includes the amount that each prospect might give, the aspect(s) of your organization's operations of the greatest interest to him or her, and other information that would be useful to the solicitors.

This anecdotal research should be followed by formal research conducted by staff or consultants. A wealth of information is now available on the Internet about individuals from all walks of life; you should be aware of the power of these research tools. Let us assume that you know that a past donor (who you believe has the capacity to make a substantially larger gift) is a businessperson, but you're uncertain about the kind of work that she does. A simple search on www.google.com might unearth loads of information on this prospect, in particular her profession. The researcher might also go on-line to do a search on your prospect in newspaper archives; on websites that specialize in biographies, such as *The Complete Marquis Who's Who*; or in on-line business directories such as the *American Medical Association* or the *West Legal Directory*. The list of informative websites goes on and on; before you contact your gift prospect, make sure your organization's staff has helped exploit these resources to the best of their ability. (Note: Zimmerman Lehman's website www.zimmerman-lehman.com includes an updated list of websites that will help you in the research effort.)[3]

Campaign Particulars

As explained earlier, campaigns (including major donor campaigns) are overseen by committees. If you are raising major gift dollars for your annual fund, we recommend convening a major gift committee to oversee the campaign. Board members and other volunteers, with the assistance of staff or consultants, form a committee to develop a strategy, theme, materials, and campaign calendar. The committee determines who the best prospects are and, having been trained to ask effectively, approaches donors with an overall dollar goal in mind. (Note the similarity to special events as described earlier: the staff "staffs" the major donor effort, and it is primarily the board members and other volunteers who ask for the gifts.)

The committee determines:

- The dollar goal of the campaign
- The amount that constitutes a major gift
- Whether to hire an outside consultant
- Who the prospects are
- Which solicitors will approach which prospects
- How to conduct research on prospects
- How to recognize donors

The committee is also responsible for preparing a campaign budget and time line, and for making sure that committee members are properly trained in the art of asking for big gifts. Even the best solicitors need some prepping, and most need a great deal. If your organization does not use a consultant for the entire campaign, you should bring someone in to instruct the solicitors on how to ask effectively. There is an art and a science to asking; training builds confidence and enthusiasm.

Once the prospects have been identified, it is important to match prospects and solicitors appropriately. Always send two solicitors to meet with a prospect; if solicitor A can't answer the prospect's question, solicitor B might. Ideally, one of the solicitors should be a friend or colleague of the prospect. If not, make sure that the solicitors and prospects are temperamentally matched. The owner of a computer start-up company with no history of philanthropy, for instance, will require a different approach than will an elderly person who has donated to nonprofits for half a century. Also, it's often a good idea to send an experienced solicitor with a rookie. This is a great way to train new board members who have never asked for a big gift.

Make sure that your organization has the means to record definitive information about prospects and about the results of solicitation visits. Review your database to see if it is sufficient. Faulty reports or poor data collection impede your ability to solicit effectively.

Once the first round of visits is completed, solicitors are responsible for reporting back to the committee and staying in touch with prospects. It is quite common for prospects to ask for additional time to consider a big gift request; they may want to speak with a spouse or significant other, visit the organization to see the staff in action, or read over the nonprofit's written materials. This is fine, so long as solicitors stay in touch in a timely—but not pushy—manner.

When the gift arrives, the executive director of the organization should send a letter of thanks, as should one of the solicitors who met with the prospect. The committee must also spend time thinking of exciting ways to recognize major donors. Listing donors' names in a newsletter and affixing a plaque to a wall is fine, but how about something more exciting? Why not host a party to thank major donors? If this is a capital campaign, a naming opportunity is a wonderful means to recognize donors.

Committee Members Must Ask for the Gifts

Your chief responsibility as a member of the major donor committee is to ask for the gifts. There are three reasons that major gift asks should be made primarily by board members and other volunteers, not by staff. First, if a staff member asks for a big gift, part of what he or she is asking for is his or her salary, and this is not the most appropriate way to solicit contributions. If, on the other hand, a board member or other volunteer asks for the gift, this is important modeling for the prospect; as a board member, you are taking the time from your busy day to meet with the prospect, who is impressed by your selflessness and dedication.

Second, as a board member, you are responsible for the governance of your organization, and prospective donors appreciate speaking with the folks who have ultimate authority. Finally, keep in mind that we want two things from a major gift prospect. We want a financial contribution, and we want him or her to be so enthused with the work of the organization that he or she will join the major donor committee next year and solicit his or her friends, relatives, and colleagues. What gives annual major donor campaigns their critical mass is more and more volunteers—who are donors themselves—joining the effort and soliciting the folks they know best. A major donor campaign therefore depends on the enthusiastic, consistent involvement of volunteers, with the support of staff members.

A final note on your responsibility as a member of the major donor committee: every committee member must make a gift to the campaign to the extent of his or her capacity. The individual you solicit for contributions won't usually ask how much you gave, but he or she may well ask whether you gave, and obviously you must be able to respond in the affirmative. Also, the more money that has been raised before kicking off the campaign, the more impressed prospects will be with the seriousness of the effort.

Since the participation of board members in pursuing major donors is so significant, we have included additional information in the Resources at the back of the book that we feel is helpful in mounting a major donor campaign. This includes specifics on how to ask for the money, an example of a typical major donor ask, and a list of campaign tasks.

EXERCISE 16

Major Gift Solicitation

Here is a detailed fictional scenario meant to help board members overcome their fear of asking and prepare them for a major donor campaign. Feel free to use a scenario based on your own organization's work.

Participants: This exercise requires a facilitator and should be done with the entire board and executive staff. The role play should be repeated by members of the major donor committee immediately prior to setting up any visits to solicit gifts.

The facilitator divides the participants into groups of four. Ideally, you should do this four times so that everyone has the opportunity to play each role.

> WomanAlive! is a domestic violence prevention organization that focuses on the problems of women who are abused by their partners. WomanAlive! provides one-on-one and group counseling, operates a shelter and a hot line for victims, and conducts public information campaigns to raise awareness of the problem of domestic violence. Since its inception WomanAlive! has offered counseling services to more than one thousand women. The mission of WomanAlive! is to educate the community about the realities of domestic violence and to serve as a source of support and safety for domestic abuse victims. By the end of this year, WomanAlive! plans to expand its activities into two neighboring counties.

> WomanAlive! staff includes an executive director, twelve paid counseling staff, a half-time development director, a half-time office manager, and forty-five volunteers. Volunteers staff the hot line and provide services at the shelter. WomanAlive!'s budget this year is $3 million. Sources include a United Way grant, grants from two local foundations and three businesses, and federal Violence Against Women Act funds. In addition, in the last year WomanAlive! mounted two direct mail campaigns and two small special events, each of which netted a moderate amount of money. WomanAlive! has never solicited contributions from major donors. By the end of this year, WomanAlive! anticipates receiving approximately $2.5 million from the sources listed here. Therefore the organization is facing a deficit by year's end of $500,000. The fourteen-member board of directors includes therapists, abuse survivors, a doctor, and a businessperson. Even though every board member makes a financial contribution, most could afford to give more than they do.

The roles:

• The WomanAlive! executive director—A social worker and longtime women's advocate, the executive director is fiercely dedicated to the work of WomanAlive! She is extremely knowledgeable about domestic violence but does not have the "clout" and connections to secure large individual contributions on her own. In this role play, it is the executive director's job to describe WomanAlive!'s mission, program, and target population, to indicate the new directions in which WomanAlive! will go in the next two years, and to field Mr./Ms. Dinero's questions and criticisms.

• The board member who is a friend of Mr./ Ms. Dinero—An old school friend of Mr./Ms. Dinero, the board member is proud to be involved with WomanAlive! (You may play this role as a therapist, volunteer, survivor,

EXERCISE 16

Major Gift Solicitation, Cont'd

doctor, or businessperson. Whichever you choose, you must have at least one rich friend: Mr./Ms. Dinero.) It is the board member's job to communicate his/her enthusiasm about WomanAlive! to the prospect and to smooth the way for the executive director. The board member should feel free to jump in with descriptions of WomanAlive! activities and comments about the importance of the mission of the organization.

• Mr./Ms. Dinero—A well-to-do local businessperson and friend of the board member, Mr./Ms. Dinero has a history of sizeable philanthropic gifts to "mainline" organizations such as the local hospital and opera company. Depending on how you choose to play this role, Mr./Ms. Dinero may be reluctant to make a contribution to a small, fly-by-night organization, or have no interest in or be actively hostile to people in abusive relationships, or claim to be overburdened by other philanthropic commitments. It is important that Mr./Ms. Dinero not be an easy sell, but also not be closed off completely to the arguments made by the executive director and the board member.

• A fourth person takes notes about key comments and body language.

After the role play, each person discusses his or her role:

- What went well?
- What was difficult?
- What clues did you get from Mr./Ms. Dinero's body language?
- Could you answer all the questions?
- Were you comfortable?
- What could you have done differently?
- Did you make the sale (that is, successfully solicit a contribution)?

The note taker reviews what he or she observed, especially the unspoken cues we all give concerning our thoughts and intentions.

If time permits, this exercise should be repeated three times more, so that every participant has the opportunity to play each role.

Time (if everyone plays four roles): Approximately one and a half hours. Each role play should take about twelve minutes, and a further ten minutes should be allowed for discussion before participants change roles.

Planned Giving

No other fundraising technique offers the dollar potential of planned giving. In a report by Boston College's Social Welfare Research Institute, it is estimated that $41 trillion in wealth will be transferred in the United States through people's estates between 2002 and 2052, of which $6 trillion will go to nonprofits.[4] This is an extraordinary amount of money. Is your organization going to get its fair share?

A planned gift, as its name implies, is a gift to a nonprofit for which plans are made in the present with an eye toward securing the gift in the future. The most common kind of planned gift—and the easiest to promote—is a bequest in a will. Other planned gift instruments are life insurance policies, charitable remainder trusts, charitable lead trusts, gift annuities, and pooled income funds. As a board member, it is not important for you to understand the particulars of these instruments. What you should understand is that planned giving allows the donor to create the means to (1) pass assets onto heirs, (2) invest in the future of his or her favorite nonprofit organization, and (3) avoid onerous taxes. If your board does not already include an estate planning attorney, you might want to add such a person and ask him or her to chair your planned giving committee.

A Few Warnings About Planned Giving

Many organizations assume that all they have to do is print up a planned giving brochure with information on various kinds of gifts and their financial value to the donor, distribute the brochure to interested parties, and sit back in anticipation of big gifts. The typical planned giving brochure, crammed with information on the joys of charitable remainder trusts, gift annuities, and pooled income funds, usually has a picture that illustrates the mission of the organization and a wan plea that "gifts from estates are vital to our future."

Organizations prepare brochures with the same old message about tax and income benefits without troubling to communicate convincingly why they need and merit planned gifts. The brochure-driven, tax-and-income-centered approach to planned giving violates basic fundraising principles. It presents no compelling case, shows no commitment from key volunteers, and relies on impersonal methods. Worse, it makes beleaguered development directors think they have to become tax and legal experts before they can start a planned giving program. Instead, your job is to put fundraising back in planned giving.

Questions for Board Members to Consider

Here are questions for board members as you consider whether to initiate a planned giving program:

- Have you already received major gifts? If not, you'll need to focus on that aspect of your fundraising before turning to planned giving.

- Does your board or development committee understand the long cultivation period necessary for a successful planned giving program? If not, have at least one member attend a planned giving seminar.

- Are you prepared to allocate resources for a planned giving program?

Creating the Planned Giving Program

The planned giving committee (made up, as is true of other committees described in this book, of board members and other interested volunteers) needs to develop a plan for the planned giving campaign, develop program protocols (types of devices used, donor recognition, and so on), and decide who will bring in technical expertise.

If your organization is just getting its feet wet with major gifts, it would be premature to launch a planned giving campaign. Once your organization feels comfortable with soliciting large gifts, you should create a planned giving committee and seek out these contributions. It's important that your major donor committee and your planned giving committee get together to vet the lists of prospective donors. You may decide that Ms. X is an excellent prospect to make a contribution toward a particular program, while Mr. Y would prefer to talk about the benefits of a charitable lead trust.

If your organization is not yet prepared to create an entire planned giving program, keep in mind that, at the very least, you can conduct a "passive planned giving campaign" by advertising for bequests in wills. Every nonprofit on earth should publish a newsletter or e-newsletter regularly, and every edition should include a display advertisement stating: "When drafting your will, please consider making a bequest to [name of your organization]." (*Please see Exercises 17a and 17b.*)

Websites and E-Mail

More and more people are spending significant portions of their waking lives glued to computer screens. This is affecting all areas of life, including philanthropy. Even though e-mail and website fundraising will not replace other fundraising techniques, they offer new and exciting philanthropic opportunities. It is the rare organization that is taking maximum advantage of what e-mail and websites have to offer. Board members can be valuable

EXERCISE 17A

If Your Organization Does Not Already Have a Planned Giving Program

Participants: This exercise requires a facilitator and should be done with the entire board and executive staff.

At a board meeting, schedule a discussion concerning initiation of a planned giving program. The facilitator informs board members that their answers to what are fairly personal questions are strictly voluntary. In fact, if you are concerned about confidentiality you can solicit this information before the meeting and furnish summaries of the responses as answers to the first two questions and the following:

- Have you made your will?
- Would you consider putting our organization in your will?

This next question is at the heart of what it takes to initiate a program:

- What would entice you to include this organization as one of your beneficiaries?

Once the answers have been compiled, give them to your development committee to determine your readiness for planned giving. This is the beginning of making the case for a planned gift contribution. It is unrealistic to assume you can start a planned gift program if no one from your board has made a planned gift.

Time: Fifteen to twenty-five minutes

EXERCISE 17B

Strengthening Your Planned Giving Program

Participants: This exercise requires a facilitator and should be conducted with the planned giving committee and development staff.

The facilitator asks the group to review your program and answer these questions:

- Where are you currently advertising your program?
- Are there other ways to let donors know they can make a donation to your organization in their will?
- Are your planned giving brochures written in plain English, or do they use a lot of sophisticated terms about legal structures used for making a donation?
- Is the case made for a contribution that goes beyond tax savings or income to the donor?
- Do you have either volunteer or paid assistance available if someone is prepared to make a planned gift?
- Have you recognized planned gift donors in your literature?

Time: Twenty-five to thirty-five minutes

players in ensuring that your organization makes good use of cyberspace fundraising.

It is not your job as a board member to design a website for your organization (unless you are technically adept and agree to volunteer your services), but it is your responsibility to ensure that the website is doing its job. Like all fundraising efforts and materials, your website must first tell your organization's story compellingly and comprehensively. Second, the site should make it desirable, easy, and secure for individuals and donors to make financial contributions. Third, the site should be kept current. Since the Internet is a speedy way to communicate, there is an understandable expectation that the site is being updated regularly. Information that is obviously dated does you no good. There are costs, then, beyond the initial design.

On-line fundraising means more than creating a website with a Donate button, which alone does not generate contributions. Imagine an individual cruising the Web looking for good causes to which to donate. Sound unlikely? It is.

What the Internet does furnish is convenience. Donors can make a gift with a few clicks of the mouse from their home or office. In fact, donors have already made millions of dollars' worth of contributions this way. But most of these on-line donations are made to high-profile or national organizations, or in response to something like a natural disaster (or in some cases "people-created" disasters such as war or terrorism). For smaller and medium-sized organizations, fundraising on the Internet is a critical part of an overall development strategy but rarely an end unto itself. The bottom line: any time you are engaging in a fundraising campaign, you should give donors the opportunity to make a gift or pledge on-line. Not every donor will take advantage of this convenience, but just like a department store thinking about its customers, you want to make it as easy and convenient as possible for donors to contribute to your worthy cause.

Cultivation

Fundraising is about building relationships. A Donate button won't do much for you in terms of cultivating your donors, but e-mail will. E-mail is a godsend for philanthropy. Your e-mail and website are excellent tools for keeping donors apprised of your organization's activities and accomplishments—for cultivation. If you have a donor's e-mail address, you can send him or her updates on your organization's activities inexpensively and effectively. Most important, you can personalize information to suit the donor's interests. The ease and cost savings of this type of communication cannot be overestimated. This opportunity was not available before, and the sooner your nonprofit takes advantage of it the better.

To begin this process your organization should be soliciting e-mail addresses in as many places as possible: your website, newsletters, membership applications, and event response cards, to mention a few. Spamming is obviously a big no-no, but most donors welcome targeted information from you, and you should always include and honor ways to opt out of any e-mail mailings.

If a donor to your health organization has expressed an interest in breast cancer, you can put her on your news alert list for breast cancer press releases but keep her off the heart disease list. Advocacy organizations are particularly effective at communicating with their supporters through alerts that request donors to take action (and that sometimes offer opportunities to donate). You can include a tag offering recipients the opportunity to donate to your organization. Here are two examples:

- Become a member of the Eastern Health Care Coalition www.eastern-healthcarecoalition.org/join

- To make a secure donation on-line to the Eastern Health Care Coalition, click this link: www.easternhealthcarecoalition.org/donate/

    Note: These are not active URLs and are used here for demonstration purposes only.

Though we believe wholeheartedly in the value of printed newsletters, you can supplement your newsletters through a handsome presentation on the Web. Web donors will probably make modest contributions initially. It is your job to upgrade these donors over the years, much as you would a direct mail donor. With cultivation, a small initial on-line contribution can turn into a major gift six years from now and a planned gift twenty years down the line. But remember: fundraising is a person-to-person business, so human contact is critical somewhere along the cultivation path.

Case Study: MoveOn.org

An example of what the Internet and on-line activities can do to raise money and awareness is MoveOn.org.[5] MoveOn.org was created by Joan Blades and Wes Boyd, two Silicon Valley entrepreneurs, during the heyday of high tech, which happened to coincide with the attempted impeachment of President Bill Clinton. The founders wanted the country to "censure and move on" past the impeachment and hence created their website. From an initial e-mail to under one hundred (three hundred) friends, MoveOn.org has grown in a few years to a virtual membership of 1.6 million nationally and 2.3 million world wide, proving that grassroots campaigns can spring from the Web.

MoveOn.org uses Web technology to motivate its members to sign petitions, make phone calls to leadership, write letters to the editor, send faxes, meet with representatives, and yes, donate money for causes or issues they support. At this writing, MoveOn.org PAC has donated more than $6.5 million to selected candidates for national office and has garnered significant media attention. If there was a world record for the most political money raised on-line in the shortest time, MoveOn.org might well claim it. In an appeal for funds to support ads about a particular issue, MoveOn.org raised over $1 million in a little over twenty-four hours from almost 20,000 donors and in three days garnered $2.3 million.

What is especially important about MoveOn.org—and what other nonprofits need to understand about Web and e-mail fundraising—is that it builds relationships with members through informational e-mails and calls to action as well as requests for donations. Not every e-mail asks for money or action; some simply provide information. MoveOn.org has the technical ability to target responses appropriately (and does) depending on stated interests, actions, or donations. (For further information on some software available for this type of customer service, see "Customer Relationship Management" later in this chapter.)

Issues to Consider Before Initiating an On-line Fundraising Program

On-line solicitations may present policy dilemmas that board members should address prior to initiating a program. For instance, there are a number of ways to solicit on-line solicitations to ensure a secure site. This may involve developing your own site with security that ensures your message, logo, and information are accurate, or to save on costs you may decide to use a service such as a charity portal (see definitions later). If you do use another organization's portal, this can raise questions about who owns the donor's information, how the donor gets thanked, and what other solicitations will be sent to the donor. How secure and private is the site? That is, how will your donor's privacy be protected by using the service or affiliation you have developed?

Another consideration: your nonprofit might decide to affiliate with a company. The company donates a percentage of the proceeds from the sale of a particular product to your nonprofit. It might turn out, however, that you deem certain other products manufactured by that company to be harmful or destructive (they could hurt the environment; they are unhealthy; they are harmful to children). Do you want your organization associated with these corporate solicitation entities? If so, do you want your donors to get solicitations from these entities?

Also, if you are accepting donations on-line, make absolutely sure that you have a system in place to document and thank the donor for his or her contribution! You must thank donors for gifts made on the Internet, and you must make sure that you are recording their e-mail addresses so you can solicit them in the future.

On-line solicitations can also raise legal or registration issues in some states, and the board should ensure that these issues are reviewed prior to starting any on-line fundraising program to be sure your organization is complying with all necessary regulations.

Terminology

There are a few terms to understand in the world of on-line fundraising.

Charity portals are websites that connect donors with a variety of charitable organizations for the purpose of making a donation on-line. Charity portals often advertise, thereby potentially attracting new donors to your cause. They may or may not charge you a fee to be listed on their site. Affiliating with a charity portal is often less expensive than setting up your own secure on-line donation system, particularly if you are just starting a program and don't expect a significant amount of donations.

Charity malls, otherwise known as "shop-to-give," are websites that allow visitors to make a purchase from a variety of businesses and donate a part of the sale to the nonprofit of their choice. Instead of going directly to the website of an on-line bookseller, for example, a charity-minded customer about to place a large book purchase might visit the charity mall first to see if the mall is linked to the book site. If that link exists, and your organization is registered with the mall, a portion (generally 2–8 percent) of the individual's purchase is given to your organization. Schools are particularly adept at using these services by promoting them to parents, especially near the holidays.

Affinity programs operate much like charity malls; nonprofits receive a small percentage of each purchase. In affinity programs, for-profit businesses use the good name of a charity to market a product. In return, the business donates a percentage of the purchase to the organization. Affinity programs often promote their products on organizational websites through a link to their own sites. Such programs might include selling anything from books to real estate.

Donate buttons can be set up directly on your site with your own secure transaction (you pay a fee and often a percentage for this service), or you can link to a charity portal to process the donation (again, usually for a fee, though some dot orgs do this for free).

Listservs are e-mail programs that enable you to send an e-mail to a large group of individuals at the same time; this is particularly useful for e-newsletters. There are free services, but they usually include their own advertising in each e-mail you send. Other listserv programs can be connected to your website and automate sign-ups and the opting-out option; they charge a fee depending on how many e-mails you send. Some fundraising software includes this capability in the application.

Customer Relationship Management (CRM) is a tool similar to a sophisticated database system that makes it easy to customize and track information about donors, members, and prospects both off-line and on-line. This tool is also called "stakeholder relationship management" software. It is especially valuable in assisting with tailoring e-mails and other forms of communication with donors or members. It can be an expensive but useful program as your fundraising becomes more sophisticated.

EXERCISE 18
On-line Fundraising

Participants: This exercise requires a facilitator and should be done with the entire board.

Before considering making solicitations on-line or initiating a relationship with an affinity program, the facilitator asks board members to discuss (or review their current) on-line solicitation policies. The answers to the questions here will help you develop or refine your policies.

- Do you want total control of on-line solicitations or are you willing to share this with another organization? (Consider the benefits of each: sharing saves money, at least initially, and is easy to set up, but you surrender some measure of control over both the presentation and what happens to donor information.)

- How secure and private is the site? (Your donors value their privacy. Can you guarantee a secure site?)

- Do you want your organization associated with any and all corporations? If so, do you want your donors to get solicitations from these entities?

- Are you currently getting the names and e-mails of donors/shoppers? If not, why not?

- Do you have an e-mail newsletter, and a way to customize or target e-mail donors' different interests?

- If you have a donor's e-mail address, can you use it for solicitation or cultivation, or must you get permission first?

- Have you explored the legal implications of soliciting donations on-line?

- Most important, do you have a system for thanking donors no matter where the gift originated?

Time: Thirty-five to forty-five minutes

Contributions from Businesses

Corporations and other businesses make contributions to nonprofits because they are genuinely interested in the work of the organization and because they believe that the contribution casts them as good corporate citizens. But what gets this ball rolling is people inside the company pitching the particular organization.

Nowhere is the fundraising rule "people give money to people" of greater importance than in the realm of business philanthropy. When we conduct a corporate and business campaign, we do not begin with formal research on prospects. Rather, we poll board members, staff members, volunteers, ex-board people, ex-staff, and other organizational intimates to find out who knows whom at local companies. It's not necessary to know the CEO (though it doesn't hurt); what we're after is the name and title of someone inside the company who would be willing to go to bat for the organization when the time comes.

Yet again, the role of the board is paramount. It's fair to say that everyone on your board of directors knows people who work in local companies, and a few board members may have connections at the highest levels. The willingness of board members to contact the folks they know at local companies is at the heart of successful fundraising from businesses.

Businesses make contributions to organizations in several ways:

- Financial contributions through a corporate foundation
- Financial contributions directly through the company
- In-kind contributions
- Matching gifts
- Event sponsorships
- Cause-related marketing
- Advertising
- Venture philanthropy

Let's briefly examine each of the ways in which a business makes philanthropic contributions.

Financial Contributions Through a Corporate Foundation

Most large corporations have formed separate philanthropic foundations. That is, the foundation has its own charter and board of directors, and it is protected to some extent from the ups and downs of the parent business. If the XYZ Fertilizer Company has a bad year, the XYZ Fertilizer Company

Foundation may do just fine that year because it has separate assets that it has invested prudently.

Corporate foundations work the way other philanthropic foundations do (see "Grantors"): they have areas of interest, guidelines, and annual reports, and many require prospective grantees to complete an application form. The only difference between corporate foundations and other kinds is that many of the former make grants to offset an organization's general expenses as well as for particular projects.

Financial Contributions Directly Through the Company

Rather than creating a separate philanthropic foundation, most small- and medium-sized companies—and even some large ones—make direct donations to nonprofits. An employee with the title of vice president for community affairs or director of corporate community relations or similar is responsible for determining which organizations to help and at what dollar level. In some instances, this employee works in concert with a small committee of other employees; in other instances, he or she works alone.

This informal arrangement makes it relatively simple for an ally of your organization inside the company to buttonhole the vice president for community affairs on behalf of your organization. Board members must tell staff whom they know at local companies.

In-kind Contributions

Some corporations prefer to make a gift of materials rather than money to a nonprofit. A company that, for example, manufactures computer software might prefer to donate product rather than cash. Also, companies are often saddled with items they no longer need but that have not outlived their usefulness. If a business decides to redecorate its offices, the old furniture may not fit the decorator's ideas but may still be of the greatest value to a legal aid program. If a large manufacturing concern upgrades its computers, the old computers may still have a lot of life left in them and be perfect for a community theater.

Matching Gifts

Many companies offer a special "perk" to employees: if an employee makes a financial contribution to a nonprofit, the company will match that gift. Usually, the match is one to one, though it is occasionally more. Here we can establish a bridge between direct mail and corporate solicitations. Direct mail letters that board members send to their friends and colleagues should indicate that many companies will match employee gifts; an employee contribution of $100 is therefore worth $200 to the organization.

Event Sponsorships

Nothing trumpets a company's status as a good corporate citizen like an event sponsorship. Whether a sit-down dinner, a day at the ballpark, or a "Las Vegas night," an event gives a company an opportunity for maximum public exposure. In our view, this is a perfectly acceptable—indeed, desirable—*quid pro quo*: the company pays for a sponsorship, and the organization emblazons the company name across the wall, on the Jumbotron screen, or wherever appropriate during the event.

An event committee must alert corporations to potential marketing opportunities. Committee members should generate a list of companies to contact that might be interested in sponsoring a golf tournament, dinner, or bike ride. Corporate websites often announce the events they have recently sponsored, thus affording you an idea of the scope of their interests. As always, make sure you use your board members' personal contacts inside a company for the best results.

Cause-related Marketing

As important as corporate philanthropic activities are to nonprofits, there is a more lucrative opportunity that awaits the most forward-thinking organizations. It stands to reason that the money a company has to dole out as philanthropic contributions is dwarfed by the resources available in its marketing department. How do nonprofit organizations gain access to corporate marketing dollars? By creating cause-related marketing opportunities.

In cause-related marketing, a company makes money through its involvement with a nonprofit. For example, a department store might take out a full-page advertisement in a local newspaper that reads: "Shop at Très Chi-Chi during the month of December, and we will donate 1 percent of your purchase to the Breast Cancer Research Fund." If you, the prospective shopper, feel that you are doing the Breast Cancer Fund some good by shopping at Très Chi-Chi, you are more likely to shop there than at a competing haute-couture emporium that has not exhibited the same desire to do good work in the community.

Other examples include a car wash that donates part of its proceeds to a local school, an ATM that donates a portion of fees to a program serving children with a debilitating disease, and a spring water company that makes a contribution to a performing arts organization for each person who signs up for home delivery. Some large nonprofits have negotiated contracts with credit card companies in which a small percentage is donated to the organization with each purchase.

One word of caution about cause-related marketing: as was the case with certain on-line fundraising programs, your organization may be viewed as endorsing a product or company through your affiliation. You must decide whether you are comfortable with this "implied endorsement." For example, thanks to government cutbacks some schools have affiliated with fast-food chains or soft-drink companies by allowing them to merchandise their products in the schools. Since child obesity has reached epidemic proportions, it begs the question of the advisability of this relationship. This is a critical policy issue with which the boards of those schools must wrestle.

Advertising

To its credit, the advertising industry has a long history of offering pro bono assistance to nonprofit organizations. For no cost (or low cost), advertising agencies "adopt" nonprofit organizations. Services might include placing a billboard trumpeting the nonprofit's accomplishments; placing a full-page advertisement in local and national magazines; preparing and placing a public service announcement on radio and television; or conferring with nonprofit board and staff members on a "full-press" marketing strategy.

A word of advice: it makes a great deal of sense to invite someone with advertising and marketing experience to join your board of directors (see "Whom to Recruit" in Chapter Four).

Venture Philanthropy

Venture philanthropy arose in the heyday of the high-tech boom. Young, socially responsible executives wanted to invest in their community by helping nonprofits build capacity and by emphasizing quantifiable performance standards. Venture philanthropy continues today, with investors bringing their own business acumen to ensuring the viability of their investments in nonprofits. One of the fastest-growing venture philanthropy groups is Social Venture Partners (SVP), which was founded in Seattle by Paul Brainerd, founder of the Aldus Corporation.

Now with affiliates throughout the United States and Canada, SVP uses a model described on their website in this way:

> *SVP Partners are individuals who want to make a meaningful contribution to nonprofit organizations—through sharing their skills, time, and financial resources. SVP invests in nonprofit organizations that seek new resources and approaches for addressing a variety of issues, including environmental protection, youth development, and education.*
>
> *The first half of the SVP model is investment that builds the long-term capacity of organizations, rather than short-term projects or programs.*

Capacity-building investments include cash grants, skilled volunteers, professional consultants, leadership development and management training opportunities. SVP Partners make an annual contribution of at least $5,000, and make decisions about how to share their collective investment. Partners provide volunteer support in areas including marketing, finance, technology, strategic planning, and human resources management. Capacity building investments contribute to increased organizational effectiveness and impact.[6]

Venture philanthropy is a growth industry in the field of corporate philanthropy; it is of great value in building effective, resourceful nonprofits that are true community enterprises.

EXERCISE 19A

Corporate Sponsorship Request

Participants: This exercise requires a facilitator and should be done with the development committee and executive and development staff.

Group members pair up for a role play. One person plays the vice president of a local corporation, and the other is a board member calling to arrange a meeting to discuss a corporate campaign. Feel free to adapt the scenario to the particulars of your organization.

Gabriele Bonds is on the board of a local gardening organization, Roses & Friends. Gabriele and Dale Small, vice president of Trash No More, are parishioners at the same house of worship. Trash No More is a major local waste management and recycling company.

Gabriele and Dale are having lunch and discussing the possibility of Trash No More sponsoring Roses & Friends' upcoming "gardening tour." Roses & Friends hires buses to take members and guests to view the most beautiful gardens in the county. This event has been very successful for the past five years and has been mentioned numerous times in the Wednesday gardening section of the local paper. There is space on the bus to advertise sponsorships, as well as on the invitation and program brochure.

After each person has played both roles, discuss these questions:

- What went well?
- What was difficult?
- As Gabriele, could you answer every question posed by Dale?
- Were you comfortable?
- Were the benefits to Dale obvious?
- Were you successful in soliciting a sponsorship?
- What might you have done differently?

Time: Thirty-five to forty-five minutes

EXERCISE 19B

Brainstorming Prospective Business Donors

Participants: This exercise requires a facilitator and should be done with the entire board and development staff.

The facilitator invites everyone to brainstorm a list of local companies and lists them on a flipchart. Next the facilitator asks each person to write down the name of any individual he or she knows who works at any of these companies, the person's job title, and the board member's connection to that person.

The development committee then prioritizes the list and discusses the ideal way in which each company might give. One company might be asked to be a sponsor; another might be solicited for a direct contribution; a third might be approached with a cause-related marketing idea. When the development committee is ready to begin its approaches, members should practice the role play in Exercise 19A.

Time: Thirty-five to forty-five minutes

Grants

Although we have emphasized the importance of setting up a comprehensive program to seek contributions from individuals and businesses, your organization certainly should not ignore the world of private and public grants. Nonprofits are eligible for grants from foundations (including corporate foundations), religious philanthropies, and agencies at all levels of government. The Foundation Center is a national organization that operates research libraries to bring to nonprofits a wealth of information about foundations and other grantors: the areas of interest of the grantor, the contact person, the average grant size, information required in letters of intent and full proposals, and more.

Private Grants

Foundations—which are themselves nonprofit organizations—are required by law to contribute a small percentage of their assets annually to nonprofits (or, in some cases, to individuals). A foundation may be established by an individual, a family, or a corporation. Many communities boast "community foundations," which combine contributions from a number of individuals and families. Foundations have particular subject areas that are dear to their hearts, and many have geographic limitations. Most of the time, foundations prefer to make grants for particular projects, not general operating expenses.

Turning to religious grantors, we note that every major faith in the United States boasts a national philanthropic program. These programs operate similarly to foundations; they too have subject areas on which they concentrate. Most religious grantors, for example, are more interested in advocacy and social welfare programs than in, say, the performing arts.

Public Grants

Agencies at all levels of government make grants to nonprofits or contract for particular services. Many nonprofits turn their noses up at government grants because they are convinced that the application process is unbearably onerous. We have found that, although proposals to government agencies may demand more time (and more "poundage") than proposals in the private sector, there is a greater opportunity for multiyear funding, often at a handsome dollar level.

The Board's Role Is Threefold

Conducting research on prospective grantors and preparing grant proposals are staff responsibilities. The board's role is threefold. First, the board must insist that staff keep them fully informed about all proposals that have been submitted to grantors. Once a proposal is submitted, staff should distribute copies to all board members. It is not at all unusual for a foundation program officer to pick up the phone to discuss the merits of a proposal with a board member at the organization. Pleading ignorance in response to such a call does not help in securing the grant.

Second, board members must grease the gears with grantors. Many folks who are new to the world of grantseeking assume that grantors consider letters and proposals solely on their merits. It is important that nonprofits submit written material that is convincing and comprehensive, but this is only half the battle. The trick, as always, is to unearth the personal contacts that ensure your proposal gets due consideration.

When, for example, our consulting firm helps an organization secure foundation grants, we always furnish members of our client's board with the names of the board members at the foundations we are pursuing. It is surprising how often a client board member says "I knew that woman in social work school and haven't seen her in years," or "We have dinner together a couple of times a year, but I had no idea he was interested in philanthropy."

As we have already described with reference to direct mail, a friendly telephone call or personal note from a board member of yours who is a friend of the foundation board member's can make all the difference.

If a national religious philanthropy receives a proposal from your local nonprofit, it stands to reason that that funder will contact someone at the local church, temple, or mosque to determine whether your organization is worthy. Board members who are also members of the congregation should talk to the head of their local house of worship to alert them to the fact that the proposal has been submitted and to reinforce the importance of your organization's work.

EXERCISE 20A

Contacts at Prospective Foundation Grantors

Participants: This exercise requires a facilitator (this can be the development director or the development committee chair) and should be done with the entire board and development staff.

This is an important exercise to do prior to submitting any grant proposal. Before conducting the exercise, the facilitator should ask staff to prepare a list of board members at foundations that your organization plans to approach. Circulate this list at the meeting and ask board members if anyone knows any foundation board members. Staff record these connections and ask our board members to call those board members as appropriate.

Time: Fifteen to twenty-five minutes

EXERCISE 20B

Meeting with a Foundation Executive

Participants: To encourage board members to follow up with colleagues or friends they know at foundation boards, have them participate in this role play. This exercise requires a facilitator (who can be the development director or the development committee chair).

This is a two-person role play. The facilitator asks one person to be a board member of a preschool and the other to be a board member of a local family foundation. You may prefer to base the role play on your own organization.

Jay Makami is an influential member of the community and a board member of a local preschool, Kids Start Right, which serves low-income families. He or she knows Pat Schneider, a board member of a local foundation, the Weir Family Foundation, whose guidelines indicate that it gives money to youth education, especially innovative learning programs for children up to age five.

Jay's two daughters attend middle school with Pat's daughter. Kids Start Right recently submitted its first proposal to the foundation for a computer-assisted teaching program for preschoolers. Jay calls Pat to let her or him know that she or he is on the board of Kids Start Right and that the organization has submitted a proposal to the Weir Foundation. She or he offers to meet for lunch and answer any questions Pat might have about the proposal or about Kids Start Right.

Discuss afterward what was easy and what was difficult about the call.

Time: Twenty to thirty minutes

The same is true with government proposals. Board members must stand ready to exercise the influence they have to convince decision makers at city, county, state, and federal agencies to give your organization's proposals a serious look.

Finally, board members must be ready to meet with grantor representatives at the grantors' behest. If a grantor is interested in your proposal, you may be invited to a visit to discuss your proposal. The grantor representative may also wish to arrange a visit to your site. In either case, the responsibility for this meeting should be shared between staff and board. The executive director or development director is almost certain to attend the meeting, but it helps immeasurably if the board president or chair of the development committee is there as well. As we saw with major donors, grantor representatives are impressed when volunteers take the time to meet with them.

Notes

1. *Giving USA*, a publication of the AAFRC Trust for Philanthropy, researched and written by the Center on Philanthropy at Indiana University.

   http://aafrc.org/

2. A nonprofit based in San Francisco, CA. http://www.homelessprenatal.org/

3. Websites for above mentioned sources of information:

   Google http://www.google.com.

   The Complete Marquis Who's Who http://www.marquiswhoswho.com/

   American Medical Association http://www.ama-assn.org/

   West Legal Directory http://lawyers.findlaw.com/

   Zimmerman Lehman http://www.zimmerman-lehman.com

4. The complete report, "Why the $41 Trillion Wealth Transfer is Still Valid: A Review of Challenges and Questions," was published in The National Committee on Planned Giving's *The Journal of Gift Planning*, Vol. 7, 1st Quarter, 2003, pp. 11–15, 47–50. The authors were John J. Havens and Paul G. Schervish of the Social Welfare Research Institute at Boston College. Full report is available at: http://www.bc.edu/research/swri/meta-elements/pdf/41trillionreview.pdf

5. A nonprofit based in Berkeley, CA. http://www.moveon.org/ (Oct. 1, 2003).

6. Social Venture Partners, a nonprofit based in Seattle, WA. To find an SVP affiliate in your community, check www.svpi.org. (Oct. 1, 2003).

Chapter 4

Effective Board Recruitment

TO ENSURE that your board has the ability to meet its responsibilities as outlined in Chapter One (planning, management, financial oversight, fundraising, legal compliance, and good governance), you need to institute a systematic recruitment policy in which you (1) identify the skills of current board members, (2) identify areas of weakness, and (3) recruit new members with skills to shore up the areas of weakness. The board nominating committee is responsible for developing and initiating a board recruitment strategy, as well as for developing a board job description, recruitment package, and orientation package. Someone with fundraising experience should serve on the nominating committee.

An effective recruitment process is vitally important to ensure the strength and comprehensiveness of your board of directors. Any professional recruiter will tell you that, when designing a recruitment strategy, the first thing to do is to identify the required skills and traits. The board nominating committee must take a close look at what is missing from your current board. In other words, you must create a profile of required skills and then identify the folks who fit that profile.

When scouting for new members, many boards give first consideration to individuals with expertise in the substantive work of the organization but with few other requisite skills. A small theater company, for example, stocks its board with individuals who have a solid grounding in theater (actors, stage designers, directors) and who can thereupon offer valuable assistance with program planning and oversight. A youth program looks for social workers and teachers; an environmental group considers people already involved in the environmental arena. This strategy is grounded in the understandable desire to gather like-minded people together in support of the organization, and this is all to the good. These board members must, however, be balanced with individuals who can play leading roles in the fundraising effort (and who, of course, are committed to the work of the organization and ready to address other board responsibilities). After all, is it fair to expect an accomplished stage designer to be an expert in fundraising and fiscal management?

When recruiting and orienting new members, most boards fail to make fundraising a priority. The ability to raise funds is rarely factored into the board recruitment process, and members are not alerted to their fundraising responsibilities. Many organizations engage in what we call "anecdotal board recruitment"—that is, current board members encourage their friends and colleagues to join the board without regard to the skills these folks possess, particularly their ability to raise funds.

Many organizations do not make the effort to convince members of the business community to become board members. They think of themselves as doing good, not making money. Yet running a nonprofit organization— be it a school, social service agency, cultural organization, or church—means running a business, though one with a charitable purpose. Raising funds is critical to the success of every business.

Let us add immediately that every board member, regardless of his or her background, can and should play a role in the fundraising effort. If a youth services agency includes a few young people on the board, they may have the capacity to move a major donor to tears by reciting their stories and showing how the agency turned their lives around. All board members can be fundraisers, but moving into fundraising high gear requires the participation of board members with money, connections, and the determination to ask.

Whom to Recruit

In addition to its program oversight and personnel responsibilities, your board must ensure that the organization has sufficient funds to carry out its mission, oversee financial record keeping and guarantee financial accountability, and promote a comprehensive program of public and media relations. To meet these responsibilities, it is vitally important to recruit new members with the requisite kinds of experience. We recommend that you recruit individuals from certain professions and walks of life to guarantee the success of your development efforts:

- *Fundraising.* People who have served as professional fundraisers or have worked as fundraising volunteers at other organizations are obviously invaluable.

- *Sales.* Salespeople make great fundraisers; they know how to make a pitch and close a deal.

- *Other kinds of businesses.* Folks in the business world (including small businesses) have skills that are useful to nonprofits, particularly if your organization engages in income-producing endeavors or charges a fee for service.

- *Public relations, marketing, and advertising.* If your organization is a well-kept secret, you won't raise much money. Folks with backgrounds in these professions will awaken your community to the importance of your work and will get you on the front page.

- *Law.* As indicated earlier in our discussion of planned giving, an estate planning attorney can jump-start your planned giving effort. Partners at big law firms are also well positioned to ask their colleagues for contributions.

- *Accounting and finance.* People from these professions understand sound record keeping, can read financial statements, and appreciate the fine points of budgets and financial plans.

- *And of course, the rich and famous.* Individuals who are movers and shakers in your community, be they entertainers, high-powered professionals, or simply people of great wealth, are central to your organization's fundraising.

You should also keep a keen eye on diversity as you develop your board, including gender, race, ethnicity, age, sexual orientation, religion, and physical difference. We feel strongly that nonprofit boards should be as diverse as the communities they serve. Diversity is also essential if your organization is to succeed with fundraising; more and more foundations, for example, fund only organizations that demonstrate diversity.

How to Recruit

We have developed the grid in Exhibit 4.1 to help you assess your current strengths and to identify areas that should be targeted in recruiting new members in the near future. Your board's nominating committee is responsible for assembling this information.

To begin your strategic board recruitment effort, the board nominating committee should fill out the grid to determine which skill areas are covered by current board members. Once the grid is complete, the nominating committee will know which skills and characteristics are missing and be able to create a profile of the person or persons to recruit next.

EXHIBIT 4.1
Board Profile Grid

	Board member name								
Skills									
Fundraising									
Sales									
Business									
Public relations									
Marketing or advertising									
Law									
Accounting or financial									
Other									
Traits and Backgrounds									
Fundraising experience									
Connections with people with money									
Connections with businesses									
Has personal wealth									
Is well known									
Has leadership skills									
Is a client representative									
Other									
Personal Characteristics									
Gender									
Race and ethnicity									
Disability									
Sexual orientation									
Age									
Religion									
Other characteristics of your community base									

The nominating committee should refine the list of skills and backgrounds with an eye toward the specific needs of your organization. Although this list includes the key elements required by most nonprofit organizations to do effective fundraising, your board may also seek other specific talents. List each board member by name. Check off each skill he or she possesses. Once you see what's missing, you'll be on your way to developing the profile for your next candidate.

The Nominating Committee

The nominating committee reviews this information and, for example, reports to the entire board in something like this way: "We have examined the backgrounds of current board members in light of our fundraising needs and have determined that our top priorities for new board members are a salesperson and a person with marketing expertise." The board then discusses these recommendations. If the full board concurs with the nominating committee, it must come up with names of particular individuals in the desired categories, in priority order. Current board members who know a particular prospect should then call to arrange a meeting to discuss the possibility of board membership.

Meet and Cultivate

When meeting with the board prospect, speak from the heart about the importance of your work with the nonprofit, describe the organization's exciting programs, and alert the prospect to plans for the future. Also, of course, inform him or her of the specific responsibilities of board membership (see the next subsection). Be sure to allow enough time to answer the prospect's questions and field his or her criticisms. If this sounds like major donor solicitation, that's because it is indeed very similar.

Allow enough time for successful cultivation. The prospect may not be ready to say yes or no at the close of your initial meeting. Leave him or her with copies of your annual report, financial statement, newsletter, and other promotional materials. Be sure to fix a date when you will get back in touch to answer questions and to find out if the prospect is truly interested in board membership. Exhibit 4.2 is a sample board member candidate form that nominating committee members and staff should fill out and present to the interviewer prior to his or her meeting with the prospect.

Remember also that interviewing someone to serve on your board of directors does not commit you to inviting that person to join. There are occa-

---

EXHIBIT 4.2
Board Candidate Form

Name of candidate:

Home address:

Home phone:

Cell phone:

Business address:

Business phone:

E-mail:

Fax:

Skills:

Current occupation:

Prior work experience:

Community or volunteer service:

Personal characteristics:

Civic and professional associations:

Prior board experience (if applicable):

Reasons I recommend the candidate for membership:

_____

_____

_____

Signature _____

---

sions when the interview reveals that, for whatever reason, the prospect would not be a welcome addition to your board. Don't be afraid to say no. If you are excessively polite, you might make a decision that will haunt your organization for years to come. Therefore be sure the prospective board member understands that he or she is being considered for membership and that the full board must vote on the candidacy. Never insinuate that the decision to join the board is the prospect's alone.

Some organizations require a prospective board member to join a committee prior to being asked to join the full board. This gives the prospect the opportunity to get to know the organization without making a significant time commitment, and it affords the organization the opportunity to determine if the prospect would indeed be a good fit for the board. Consider asking your prospect to serve on your special events or fundraising committee to assess her or his aptitude and interest in service to your board.

Job Description

To recruit new members effectively, your board of directors should have a written board member job description. A sample checklist for a job description is included in the following bulleted list. Prospective board members should understand their responsibilities prior to signing on. If, for example, a prospect bridles at the idea of giving money and soliciting colleagues for contributions, he or she probably does not belong on your board. Also, be clear about what specific responsibilities this particular board member will have. If you have decided that your highest priority is finding a lawyer with an estate planning background, alert the prospect to the fact that he or she will be expected to join the planned giving committee. Understand of course that said lawyer will not be financially compensated for any work that he or she does as a board member.

Every member of the board of directors is expected to:

- Attend regularly scheduled board meetings.

- Review minutes and stay well informed regarding the organization's fiscal and program work.

- Participate in setting overall policy.

- Participate actively on at least one committee.

- Participate in an annual planning retreat.

- Make an annual financial contribution from personal resources, to the extent of capacity.

- Approach colleagues and friends for contributions through such activities as selling tickets for special events and appending notes to fundraising letters.

- Take responsibility for overseeing the organization's finances.

- Speak on behalf of the organization to the community.

- Participate in an annual evaluation of the executive director.

- Avoid conflicts of interest.

- Agree to participate without financial compensation.

New Member Orientation

Once the prospect decides to join the board, it is crucial to orient him or her appropriately and comprehensively. Present the new member with a board package containing these items:

☐ Job description

☐ Mission statement

☐ Bylaws

☐ History of the organization and its programs

☐ Sources of the organization's funding

☐ Annual report

☐ Website information

☐ Organization's policy manuals

☐ Current budget and the most recent audit statement

☐ Strategic and development plans

☐ Organization chart and job title or description with names of staff

☐ Roster of current board members and contact information

☐ List of officers, as well as committee chairpersons and committee members

☐ Organization newsletters and brochures

☐ Minutes from the three most recent board meetings

For people who are new to nonprofit boards, we recommend their attending a training in board responsibilities. You might want to mount this training yourself or send the new board member to an organization specializing in providing technical assistance to nonprofit volunteers. Also, it helps to appoint a "buddy" for the new board member. The buddy is a current board member whose job it is to introduce the new member to everyone on the board, and to answer the questions that inevitably arise. Make sure that the buddy checks in with the new member after a few months to find out if the new member feels he or she has sufficient information to begin making informed decisions.

Chapter 5

Primed for Fundraising

NOW THAT YOU HAVE a clear sense of the board's role in fundraising and the most effective means to recruit new members who can help with this all-important effort, it's time to consider what else your organization needs to guarantee success. These essential elements are a comprehensive development plan, trained and dedicated staff, organizational leaders who understand their responsibilities (the board chair, development committee chair, executive director, and director of development), a fundraising budget that accurately reflects the cost of doing business, appropriate use of consultants, and a plan for evaluating your nonprofit's development effort.

Creating a Development Plan

The best fundraising is done systematically, not episodically. This requires a development plan, which is a blueprint for raising the funds required to achieve the goals stated in your strategic plan. It is the board's responsibility to direct staff to prepare a fundraising plan, or to commission a consultant to do so. If your board decides to hire a consultant, fundraising committee members must work with the executive director and development director in the selection process. If you choose to proceed without a consultant, the fundraising committee must help staff determine strategies and set goals. The staff is then responsible for drafting the plan for the committee's review. Once the plan is completed, the fundraising committee is responsible for monitoring the implementation of the plan and reporting to the full board on developments.

The persons responsible for the plan begin their assessment of your organization's fundraising efforts by interviewing a cross-section of board members, staff members, donors, and other organizational intimates to secure their opinions concerning the quality of the fundraising work. The only drawback to using a staff member in this capacity rather than a consultant is that interviewees may be reluctant to be as forthright with their opinions as they would be in talking with an objective third party.

Assessing Your Fundraising to Date

The persons preparing the plan begin with a review of all relevant written material, including letters of intent, full proposals, direct mail letters, special events programs, case statements, annual reports, brochures, and other fundraising and promotional written material. Once they have completed this review, the folks preparing the plan interview twelve to fifteen organizational intimates. Interview questions, which are asked in complete confidence, should include these:

- Why did you get involved with this organization?
- What are your specific responsibilities as a staff (or board) member or volunteer?
- How good a job does the organization do in keeping board members and other volunteers apprised of activities, upcoming events, and changes in programs?
- What is your opinion of the services offered to clients?
- How effective has the board been in raising funds?
- How effective has the staff been in communicating its need for fundraising assistance to the board?
- How good a job does the organization do with regard to media and public relations?
- What is your opinion of the quality of the research that the organization does with regard to grantors, including foundations, corporations, religious donors, and government agencies?
- With reference to the most recent direct mail campaign, what did you think of the letter and enclosures? Did board members and volunteers append personal notes to letters? Were the letters mailed in a timely fashion? Do you have other comments about the direct mail campaign?
- What is your opinion of the most recent special event? How successful was the organization in selling sponsorships? Did attendees appear to be excited and involved? What did you think of the speaker? The food? The music? Was registration handled intelligently? What did you think of the locale? Do you have other comments about the event?
- How would you rate the most recent major donor campaign? Were the solicitors well trained? Did they make their pitches to prospects effectively? Were the written materials that were presented to prospects attractive and compelling?
- Does the organization take full advantage of e-mail and the Web in fundraising? If not, what might they do?

- (Asked of board members and other volunteers) When the organization approached you for a contribution, was it done by mail? in person? by phone?

- Who asked for the gift? Did you make a gift? How might the solicitor have been more effective in his or her approach?

Armed with information culled from the review of materials and the interviews, the people preparing the plan are ready to write an assessment of your organization's fundraising to date. The assessment includes a detailed evaluation of all fundraising and public relations activities undertaken by the organization in the recent past (usually three years), with particular emphasis on the board's enthusiasm for fundraising and the adequacy of staff time devoted to fundraising and public relations.

Sample Board Fundraising Evaluation

An important part of the assessment is an evaluation of the board's involvement in fundraising. Here is a sample board evaluation section of a fundraising plan.

Greener America Board Fundraising Evaluation

Greener America came within $10,000 of meeting its overall fundraising goal in the last fiscal year. The board concentrated its fundraising efforts on selling tickets to the Forests Forever Luncheon and succeeded in selling tickets to friends, relatives, and colleagues. Board members also purchased tickets to the Organic First breakfast and made thank-you calls to donors. The board has helped, occasionally and sporadically, by setting up meetings with grantors and attending major donor cultivation events. Board members have not, however, scoured their lists of friends and colleagues and asked them for big gifts. The board also has not provided Greener America with a list of more modest prospects to receive direct mail letters; nor have board members appended personal notes to direct mail letters as appropriate. Although some board members have assisted Greener America by opening the door for corporate contributions and sponsorships, more could be done in this area as well.

Here is an assessment of Greener America's special event.

Let's turn to the Forests Forever Luncheon. On December 12, Greener America held its tenth annual Forests Forever Luncheon at the Downtown Main Street Hotel. The luncheon was attended by over 800 people and grossed in excess of $450,000. The Greener America staff—particularly Ms. Belinda Bay Leaf and Mr. Carlos

Cumin—deserve heartiest congratulations for an event that boasted the following:

- Registration that was organized and did not keep people waiting
- A lively pre-lunch cocktail party
- Great food
- A program that was engaging and informative, and that ended on time
- Delightful gift bags that guests took home with them

Belinda put together a detailed calendar with tasks for every month beginning in January. (For the Organic First event, she prepared a similar calendar for June through October.) After the luncheon, Belinda prepared a long memorandum, "Suggestions for Improvement for Next Year's Forests Forever Luncheon," with specific "marching orders" for next year's event.

While attendance and gross revenue did not increase between last year and this year, the tighter economy this year meant that holding the line constituted a substantial victory.

We have one major concern about the luncheon: though events can and should make money, another important purpose is to capture people so as to solicit them again and again. The person who attends the luncheon may well be interested in making an additional contribution via direct mail, or becoming a major donor, or making a planned gift when the time comes. If Greener America doesn't capture these individuals, such opportunities go out the window.

When a corporation buys a Forests Forever Luncheon table, Greener America gets the names of the people at the table, but no other contact information. Greener America does not therefore have the ability to pursue these individuals for contributions in future months and years. How can Greener America capture these folks without seeming unduly intrusive?

One suggestion is to have cards at each table that attendees can fill out to subscribe—free of charge, of course—to Greener America's excellent newsletter. The master or mistress of ceremonies will be instructed to alert folks from the podium that these cards are at the tables. Not everyone will fill them out, of course, but enough will do so to allow Greener America to get these individuals' names, addresses, telephone numbers, and e-mail addresses into its database. This may seem minor but is not. If even one person so captured makes a major gift to Greener America or names Greener America a beneficiary in a charitable remainder trust, the effort will have been worthwhile.

Proposing New Strategies for Fundraising

After the assessment is complete, the second step is to propose new or expanded development strategies not yet initiated by the organization. For example, in assessing Greener America the persons writing the plan concluded that the organization was quite successful with direct mail but needed to move some of these modest donors into the category of prospective major donors.

> Greener America has ignored the potential that lies in face-to-face solicitation. The only face-to-face asking that Greener America has done was during the capital campaign three years ago. These asks— which were done primarily by the executive director and the director of development—were highly successful; Greener America generated significant support and these visits helped push the capital campaign over its $7 million goal. Greener America has not, however, built on this success. It is time that face-to-face major gift solicitation become part of Greener America's annual campaign and that the board of directors get involved in the solicitations.

> Greener America could be raising significantly more money if donors with significant capacity were asked for gifts in person. They could be named members of the "Forest Club." Most donors give to nonprofits because the right person asks and because the donor cares about the organization, but there is no question that perks help. The Forest Club could offer some perks, including recognition of major gifts in a variety of formats and guided tours of Greener America parkland projects.

> The foundation has been laid, then, for an annual, in-person major donor campaign. What must be emphasized here is that volunteers need to join with staff if the campaign is to be successful. The major donor committee will be composed of members of Greener America's board of directors, other volunteers from the community who love Greener America and who have connections to major donor prospects, the executive director, the director of development, and the director of major gifts.

> Board members and other volunteers are important to this effort because their involvement speaks volumes about their dedication to the goals and mission of the organization. Once the prospect makes a gift, it will be Greener America's job to continue to cultivate that person with two goals in mind for the second year: to solicit another gift and to encourage that donor to join the major donor committee himself or herself. Thus, if the major donor campaign becomes part of Greener America's annual campaign, the

effort will grow from year to year because a certain percentage of donors in year one will become solicitors in year two. These new solicitors will open their lists of connections and the prospect list will grow. There is no reason not to start today.

The Fundraising Calendar

The final and most important section of the fundraising plan is the task list calendar. The calendar includes a semiannual list of responsibilities within each fundraising category. Included are the particular tasks in each category, the person or persons responsible for those tasks, and the financial goal. The plan is a user-friendly document that can be conveniently displayed above the desks of every board member, the executive director, the development director, and other appropriate individuals. (*See Exhibit 5.1.*)

In preparing the fundraising calendar, how do we come up with dollar goals in each category?

- The goal should represent something of a stretch—not so high as to risk failure nor so modest as to be too easily attainable.

- The goal should be based on the ability to raise the money, not on the need for the money. If it will cost $10 million to build and outfit a new building, a goal of $10 million makes sense only if the capital campaign feasibility study indicates that that much money can be raised.

- The intimates of the organization—board, staff, volunteers, families of clients—should be the landmark donors. When estimating goals, think first of how much the intimates might give.

There is no magic formula for setting the dollar goal. Consider how much a particular campaign netted last time and whether circumstances have changed to merit an increase in the dollar goal. For instance, is a past major donor nearing retirement, someone who might give serious consideration to leaving a $1 million bequest to your organization and therefore increasing your planned giving revenues 25 percent? Will this year's special event include a well-loved keynote speaker who will drive up your attendance 50 percent? Have you doubled the size of your development office, thereby increasing the amount of time that staff can devote to preparation of foundation proposals?

With regard to particular fundraising strategies, here are a few useful rules of thumb in determining dollar goals:

- *Special events.* Assume that you will mail eight invitations to individuals for every ticket that is purchased.

- *Major donors.* At the top levels (the top of your donor pyramid), you must make five asks for every gift; at the middle levels, four asks for every gift; and at the bottom levels, three asks for every gift.

- *Direct mail.* In campaigns aimed at folks who have never given to your organization, a return rate of 1.5 percent or better is excellent.

These are conservative estimates, and we certainly hope that your nonprofit exceeds them by a considerable margin.

Here is an example of the Major Donor and Foundation sections in Greener America's calendar.

> The first major donor campaign, which will be aimed at raising funds to offset Greener America's annual operating expenses, will be conducted in year two of this calendar. In year one, Greener America will lay the groundwork for the campaign.

What the Board Needs to Understand About Fundraising Staff

Too few board members understand how terribly labor-intensive fundraising is. They lobby executive directors to keep their operations "lean and mean," thereby effectively cutting themselves off at the fundraising knees.

It is the rare organization that has enough fundraising staff. A major university may employ 150 people in its fundraising office but need 200; a small, community-based counseling program expects the executive director to cover all the fundraising bases without so much as a part-time administrative assistant.

The optimum size of a fundraising office is not a function of an organization's overall budget. We know of a $50 million medical research project funded by two grants from the National Science Foundation that does not require a full-time fundraiser (a part-time proposal writer does nicely). On the other hand, a pediatric cancer clinic with an annual budget of $5 million that raises funds via foundation grant proposals, corporate solicitations, direct mail letters, sales of tickets to special events, major donor visits, and planned gift efforts requires enough staff to address all areas comprehensively.

Cultivation of prospective donors takes time and effort and cannot always be measured in dollars and cents, especially when an organization is new to the world of individual giving. As explained earlier, the thank-you letter sent to the donor in response to his or her first gift is the first step in getting the second gift. Organizations require fundraising staff to solicit initial grants and contributions and to cultivate donors consistently and imaginatively in securing future contributions. It is the rare organization that does enough cultivation because it is the rare organization that has enough staff to cover all the fundraising bases.

EXHIBIT 5.1

Fundraising Category: Major donor campaign
Time Period: January 1, [year 2] to June 30, [year 2]
$$ Goal: $150,000

Tasks	Responsible Parties
Convene the major donor committee.	Board chair, development committee
At the first meeting of the committee, discuss the importance of major gifts to Greener America's fiscal health, and provide names of others who might join the committee. Elect a chair.	Major donor committee
Invite these prospective committee members to the next meeting (approximately one month later).	Committee chair and director of major gifts
At the second meeting, draft campaign timetable and discuss how Greener America will sell its work to prospects.	Director of major gifts and major donor committee

Fundraising Category: Foundations
Time Period: January 1, [year 2] to June 30, [year 2]
$$ Goal: $100,000

Tasks	Responsible Parties
Complete research profiles of the best prospective foundation grantors.	Director of development
Prepare first draft of letter of intent to foundations.	Director of development, with input from the executive director
Review board members at foundations with Greener America's board to determine who knows whom.	Director of development, executive director, and entire board

Good fundraising means targeted marketing, and targeted marketing is labor-intensive. As indicated earlier, the most effective direct mail campaigns target particular constituencies and amend the text of the letters to agree with the interests of those constituencies. A successful major donor campaign depends on extensive research to determine not simply how much someone might contribute but what his or her political slant is and which hot button issues might crop up during the face-to-face visit. Nonprofits need labor power to generate this information.

As a board member, your job is not to hire fundraising staff (unless invited to serve on an interview panel by the executive director) but to help the executive director determine the size of the fundraising office and budget, and the appropriate positions within the office.

What Development Staff Can and Cannot Do

When a development director leaves to seek other employment, the most common reason for his or her defection is not that the pay is too low or the accommodations too spartan. In our experience, the primary reason is that the board and the executive director offer little support and have no conception of what a development director can realistically be expected to do.

To promote harmony and short-circuit conflict among your board members, executive director, and development staff, we recommend first that your organization develop detailed job descriptions for development staff (and, of course, for board members, as described earlier). As a board member, it is crucial that you understand what a development staff person is expected to do. For example, if your organization is of relatively modest size and has a one-person fundraising office, board members should realize that the development director is responsible for a host of activities, from putting out direct mail letters and newsletters to preparing foundation grant proposals, running major gift campaigns, and supervising volunteers.

The board must also be realistic about the amounts that can be raised from specific fundraising activities. For example, a board member of a small community music school attends a gala at the local symphony that nets $500,000. The board member calls the development director at the music school and waxes euphoric about the symphony's event. "We may not have access to as many deep pockets as the symphony," the board member says, "but we certainly should be able to raise $250,000 at our upcoming cocktail party, right?"

Wrong. With no wealthy people on the board and only a modest number of past donors, the music school will be fortunate to raise $20,000. Board members must understand what is realistic without losing sight of the possibility of raising huge dollars a few years down the road.

Development staff also experience frustration with board members who exhibit enormous initial enthusiasm about fundraising projects but who fail to follow through on their tasks. The development plan described earlier establishes a structure to ensure that tasks are addressed, but someone must be responsible for nudging board members to do what they have committed to do.

Some organizations rely on the development director to guarantee that fundraising tasks are addressed on time and in full. Others find that board members resent being told what to do by staff; in such a case, the chair of the development committee should ride herd on board members and other volunteers or should seek the assistance of a consultant.

Specific Fundraising Roles

For effective fundraising there are a number of key positions. We elaborate on what these are and some important tasks they should perform.

Chair of the Board

Successful fundraising requires the active and enthusiastic participation of the chairperson of your board. He or she is responsible for setting the tone for a true "culture of philanthropy" in your organization. The chairperson first must make a financial contribution to your organization that is truly a stretch gift. He or she should also address the board and inform members of their fundraising responsibilities.

Most important, the chairperson of your board must visit each board member in person to ask for a capacity gift to your organization. It is a serious mistake to solicit these gifts by letter or—even worse—to make a speech at a board meeting and expect board members to send donations at their convenience. Solicitation of board gifts is identical to solicitation of major gifts: the asks must be made in person. Your board president should also be ready to meet with major donor prospects and with personnel from foundations, corporations, and other grantor agencies. Donors and grantors will certainly want to speak with the executive director; they will also appreciate the involvement of your top volunteer, the board chair.

Fundraising Committee Chair

Like the board chair, the fundraising committee chair is responsible for establishing and maintaining a culture of philanthropy in your organization. The chair must ensure that the committee is made up of enthusiastic fundraisers who understand that fundraising is not genteel begging but rather creation of opportunities to invest in your community. The chair's job is to make sure that fundraising committee members meet their responsibilities as described in the plan calendar. As we have already noted, the fundraising committee chair may also have the larger job of leaning gently on board members and other volunteers to guarantee that they complete their fundraising tasks.

Executive Director

Although Zimmerman Lehman has met the occasional executive director who is fond of fundraising, most do not view fundraising as their primary responsibility. They either (1) avoid fundraising like the plague and feel guilty about failing to ensure their organizations' financial future or (2) spend all their time doing fundraising and are angry that they've been dragged away from the program work of their organization.

What is the executive director's fundraising role? Directors should not be expected to do the numerous day-to-day tasks required for successful fundraising. Writing thank-you letters, designing event invitations, making sure that direct mail letters are back from the printer on time: these are not executive director responsibilities but more properly belong to development staff. If yours is a small organization that does not have development staff, you should explore outsourcing certain fundraising jobs.

The executive director's fundraising role is as the front person. He or she—often in the company of the board president—meets with foundation presidents, escorts major donor prospects around the organization's premises, and signs direct mail letters. The executive director is the person who comes most readily to mind when the donor thinks of your organization.

For those organizations that have a development staff, it is their job to position the executive director in the fundraising effort. "On October 6th," the director of development of California Youth Connection might say to the executive director, "you and the board president have an appointment to meet the president of the Philanthropy Tomorrow Foundation to discuss our youth leadership training program." Naturally, the executive director should be aware of the details of the program and review the proposal prior to the meeting.

The executive director has an additional fundraising responsibility: to supervise the development director. The savvy executive director understands that, in evaluating the work of the development director, the amount of money that he or she has raised is not the primary criterion. More important is the number of fundraising opportunities created. If the development director implements a variety of fundraising strategies appropriately and conscientiously, the organization will generate income. Too many executive directors assume that development directors should earn twice or three times their salary as a measure of success. This is simply unrealistic; fundraising, as we noted earlier, is not a quick-fix business. If the development director does the job right—and if he or she gets the full cooperation of the board of directors—the fundraising effort will succeed in the long run.

Development Director

The title "development director" means so many things to different organizations that it is virtually robbed of meaning. In some organizations, the development director does little more than prepare grant proposals; in others, he or she is responsible for ten fundraising programs. Some development directors work with a staff of fifty; others are a one-person shop.

Regardless of the size of an organization's fundraising operation or the variety of its fundraising approaches, certain things are true for the huge majority of development directors:

- The development director builds and maintains fundraising systems. He or she keeps an eye on the fundraising plan and confers regularly with the executive director, board chair, and fundraising committee chair to make sure all tasks are addressed in a timely and appropriate way.

- He or she positions the executive director to assist with fundraising by, for example, scheduling meetings with foundation presidents and major donor prospects or arranging for the executive director to speak at the monthly meeting of a civic organization.

- He or she supervises fundraising staff and assures completion of all research, writing, and promotional activities. In a one-person shop, the development director is responsible for all grunt work.

- In concert with the executive director, the development director meets periodically with the full board of directors to apprise its members of fundraising activities.

Fundraising Costs

There are no set "prices" or rates of return for particular fundraising activities. An organization new to direct mail, for example, will do well to break even on its first drop. An organization that has conducted direct mail campaigns for fifty years, on the other hand, can and should expect a significant profit from campaigns targeted at current donors (but not at new prospects).

An organization that mounts its first special event may realize a very modest return but should take comfort in the fact that it has captured attendees who will, as described earlier, be pursued in the future via direct mail and other fundraising approaches. A nonprofit that is holding its tenth annual luncheon, however, had better be making money.

Our point is that, when it comes to pricing fundraising activities, one size does not fit all; there is no magic formula to help the board determine whether its fundraising is cost-effective. That said, board members should certainly pay attention to fundraising costs. The fundraising committee should ask the development director to prepare quarterly reports containing detailed information on the cost of doing fundraising business.

Budget Items

Sample costs for a fundraising budget include, under the heading of general fundraising expenses:

Salaries

Postage

Telephone and fax

Supplies

Printing and copying

Travel

Memberships and professional expenses

Subscriptions and books (on-line, data research, and so on)

Training

Consulting fees

Computers

Fundraising software

Overhead (space, equipment, insurance, and so forth)

Expenses for particular fundraising activities include:

Printing and copying

Postage

Site costs (rental of a banquet room, for instance)

Food

Technical assistance, such as mailing houses or list brokers

Graphic designers

Music

On-line expenses

Advertising

Donor plaques and other recognition items (goodie bags for event attendees)

Even though we strongly caution against judging the success or failure of specific fundraising activities in terms of revenue versus costs, we do feel that these activities must become more cost-effective over time. Making a modest amount of money on your first telephone solicitation campaign is perfectly acceptable; making only a modest amount on your twelfth such campaign is unconscionable.

Working with Consultants

Nonprofit staff and board members must be ready to shoulder their share of fundraising responsibilities, but it is appropriate in some instances to outsource a portion of the development work. Organizations large and small have crafted successful relationships with fundraising consultants. Consultants may specialize in a particular type of fundraising (special events, direct mail, major gifts) or may offer a variety of services under the same roof (often for large capital and endowment campaigns).

To foster a successful relationship with a fundraising consultant, nonprofit board and staff members should:

- Convene a small committee composed of the executive director, the director of development (if your organization has one), and one or two board members to decide upon the appropriate consultant.

- Determine which fundraising approaches are appropriate for your organization but have not been implemented for lack of staff time (see "Evaluating Your Fundraising Effort" later in this chapter).

- Contact your local chapter of the Association of Fundraising Professionals to secure names of reputable consultants in the subject areas in which you need help.[1]

- Speak with folks at other nonprofits who have worked with consultants to unearth additional prospects

When interviewing consultants, keep in mind that the person or firm must have impeccable professional credentials and must be an appropriate fit for your organization. It is obviously important to ascertain that the consultant has a wealth of experience in your area of interest; references are therefore vital. In determining whether the consultant fits your organization, the committee members must be honest with themselves, by being asked: When the prospective consultant made his or her sales pitch, did you feel discomfited? enthusiastic? bored? Did you have a hard time imagining this consultant working harmoniously with your board? Did the three-piece suit and silky delivery make you queasy? Remember: you want the professional experience, but you also want a person or firm that will complement your organization's personality.

If the interview goes well, request a proposal from the consultant enumerating specifically what that person or firm will do (and, if it is a firm, who from the firm will be doing the work), what your staff and volunteers are expected to do, when the major tasks are to be accomplished, and what the consulting assistance costs. With reference to cost, we are proponents of a straight fee rather than a percentage of the money raised. Many organizations assume that percentage-based fundraising would leave them off the hook were no money to be raised. We believe that percentage-based fundraising borders on the unethical; if fundraising consultants make the front page, it is usually because they have been accused of keeping an obscene percentage of the money they raised. In an article entitled "The Ethics of Consulting Fees," the Association of Fundraising Professionals puts it well: "Percentage-based compensation encourages abuses, imperils the integrity of the voluntary sector, and undermines the very philanthropic values on which it is based." It is good business for the organization to know the services it is buying and for the consultant to secure a respectable fee for his or her services.

Evaluating Your Fundraising Effort

The board fundraising committee, in concert with the executive director and the development director, is responsible for conducting an annual evaluation of your organization's fundraising effort. Keep in mind that you are focusing on money raised and on opportunities created. Here are examples of the questions you should ask, in a variety of categories. First, for the board of directors and other volunteers:

- Did the board meet its fundraising goals?

- Did every board member give to his or her capacity?

- How many current members of our board of directors are trained and enthusiastic fundraisers?

- Are volunteers other than board members assisting with our organization's fundraising effort?

Questions for fundraising staff:

- Did staff address all tasks outlined in the fundraising plan in a timely manner?

- Does our organization require additional staff to ensure the success of the development effort?

- Did the written materials make the case effectively?

- Did donor records provide sufficient information to enable solicitors to ask for gifts effectively? Does our fundraising database have the capacity to record gifts, store information from solicitors about interviews, and mail merge for direct mail and e-mail correspondence?

Regarding specific fundraising efforts, there are representative questions to ask about particular techniques and fundraising tools. Your committee can pick and choose among them and should prepare other questions in light of your fundraising plan goals. Let's begin with direct mail:

- Were the letters and enclosures compelling?
- Did past donors receive letters that acknowledged their most recent gifts and that asked for more?
- Did board members furnish their list of contacts?
- Did board, staff, and other intimates of your organization append personal notes to friends and colleagues?
- Were you making proper use of list brokers to secure lists of prospects?
- Did you mail often enough?
- Was the mailing house that was responsible for the mail drop dependable and punctual?

Questions regarding events:

- Did your events attract enough attendees?
- Did you charge enough money?
- Did you create opportunities for attendees to learn more about your organization?
- Did your events end on time?
- Did you follow up with attendees (for instance, by adding them to your direct mail list)?
- Did board members invite all their contacts?
- Did all board members attend?
- Are fundraising staff burned out by events?

Questions on major donors and planned gift donors:

- Did the major or planned gift committee do a good job of identifying prospects? in training solicitors? in matching solicitors and prospects?
- Were the written leave-behind materials pertinent and handsome?
- Did solicitors follow up with prospects in a timely manner?
- Was the campaign dollar goal too modest? too high?
- Were the solicitors trained effectively?

- Did the solicitors have adequate information about prospects before visiting them?

- Did the solicitors do an effective job of asking? What worked? what didn't? What did you learn for next time?

Questions about grantors:

- Did the fundraising office conduct comprehensive research at the Foundation Center library and on-line to unearth all prospective grantors, including foundations, corporations, religious grantors, and agencies at all levels of government?

- Did the letters of intent, applications, and full proposals convey the importance of our organization?

- Did they lay out specific information about the projects for which funding was sought?

- Did they reflect the particular interests of each grantor?

- Did board members identify foundation, corporate, and government contacts and follow up by making phone calls and appointments?

Questions regarding on-line solicitations:

- Does your website make it easy for donors to contribute?

- Does the website give donors and other readers information about your organization that is comprehensive and attractive?

- Did staff put e-mail to use in cultivating donors by sending regular e-mail newsletters?

Finally, questions about your database:

- Was your fundraising software effective?

- Was your software user-friendly, or did it drive administrative staff crazy?

- Did the reports that were generated offer sufficient detail to allow analysis of costs and profits?

Once the committee has made its evaluation, it should be presented to the entire board and discussed in detail. Your fundraising plan should be amended in light of what the evaluation indicates.

Note

1. Association of Fundraising Professionals is a professional association with its national office located in Alexandria, VA. http://www.afpnet.org/

Conclusion

A GENTLE REMINDER, finally: even in tough times, the money is there. People are honored to be asked, and thrilled to give. Your love and respect for your organization will close the sale, and you will raise all the money you need to guarantee that your organization survives and prospers. As board members who by now should be enthusiastic fundraisers, you are giving people an opportunity to feel good about themselves through philanthropic gifts and to invest in your successful community enterprise.

We close with a success story that is a lesson to everyone who reads this book. Our son, Gabe, attended a wonderful preschool in Berkeley, California, called Step One School.[1] When we enrolled Gabe at Step One and inquired about fundraising (other than tuition), we discovered that the school's main activity was a dinner with an auction that required countless staff and volunteer hours (the school had no development director; the codirectors did all of the staff fundraising work) and netted a pittance. Occasionally a board member would send a friendly holiday letter that would garner a few donations. No follow-up, no tracking of donors, and an event that grew more burdensome each year, burning out many folks along the way.

Colleges, universities, and independent schools had used a variety of fundraising strategies for years—most preschools did not, and Step One was no exception. Conversations with board and staff members furthermore revealed little fundraising experience and serious fear and loathing about asking for money. The codirectors and the board feared rejection, and they were concerned that fundraising would create "class issues" that would ruin their inclusive community. That is, parents of moderate means would, they worried, be treated as second-class citizens. One board member also equated fundraising with "prying."

We began our efforts at Step One by meeting with staff and board to plan a more diversified fundraising strategy and by conducting a series of trainings for the school's board of directors. Through the use of certain of the exercises found in this book, we moved board members—and the codirectors—past their fears. We reviewed the wonderful work of the teachers and school and demonstrated that tuition alone could never cover all the school's expenses (especially if preschool teachers were to be paid a worthy wage). The board members and volunteers realized that there might indeed be a few people who could subsidize the rest by making larger donations. These individuals could be honored along with others who devoted time and energy to Step One, and the school could also hold community events that would be inclusive of everyone.

We also emphasized follow-up with those who did give (including alumni and grandparents), research on potential donors, publication of newsletters, and practice in making the ask. The school initiated a formal annual campaign via letter and a major donor campaign. The first few major donor asks, though difficult, elicited significant sums, and this encouraged the other solicitors to soldier on. The annual campaign also grew each year and a larger portion of alumni made gifts. Within six years, the annual campaign was netting close to $100,000; parents, board members, and staff had become accustomed to and comfortable with asking and giving; askers felt "they were doing donors a favor" by creating opportunities to give; and donors felt honored to be able to help this wonderful institution that did such a great job teaching their young children.

The school began an endowment fund for teachers and a capital campaign for a novel educational garden for preschoolers, and they turned their formerly exhausting fundraising event into a simpler community event for all. When we asked what the key was to Step One's success, one of the codirectors replied: "We learned how to ask for the money."

So remember these key points for successful fundraising:

- Ask for the money in as many ways as appropriate (diversification, similar to a good financial investment plan)

- Keep the donor in mind (good donor/customer relations, cultivation, and appreciation)

- Focus on the worthy cause of giving donors the opportunity to invest in your successful community enterprise (your nonprofit business/mission)

Do this, and we promise you the money will follow!

Note

1. A nonprofit based in Berkeley, CA. http://www.steponeschool.org/

Resource A

Major Donor Solicitation: Asking for the Gift

Who Should Do the Asking?

You must decide who will approach the prospect and how much to request. Remember: people give money to people. The person who is closest to the prospect should contact him or her by phone to arrange a meeting. If the prospect is not personally known to anyone at your program, choose the volunteer or staff member whose interests and background best reflect those of the prospect.

How Do You Cultivate the Prospect?

Keep in mind that major donor solicitation is a process of cultivation; it may take weeks before you are able to arrange an appointment to meet a prospect, and it may take three or more meetings before the prospect is ready to talk about a large contribution. Do not rush to judgment. If the prospect is not ready this year, you must think long-term. Perhaps he or she needs to become better acquainted with your organization. Put him or her on your newsletter list, invite the person to a special event, and consider asking him or her to be a committee or board member. Keep the cultivation process going (unless you get some indication that your efforts will be wasteful). Take the time that it requires to cultivate a prospect effectively.

How Do You Make the Appointment?

Do not make a major gift request over the phone. Do not accept a small contribution offered by the prospect by phone. Insist—politely but firmly—on getting together face-to-face. You might say something like: "Our organization has expanded considerably in the past eighteen months. We'd like to get together sometime in the next two weeks to fill you in on our new projects and to explore the ways that you might help us in the coming year."

Two people from your organization should visit the prospect: the person who made the phone call, and a second person who has extensive and substantive knowledge of the work of your organization. (The executive director is often a good choice, but don't burn out the executive director by asking him or her to attend forty solicitations. Two board members should be able to handle a major donor visit on their own.) Both askers must be passionate about and committed to the work of the program, and they should be good listeners.

Turning now to the particulars of the ask, let's assume that the prospect is a friend of a member of your organization's board of directors. The board member has phoned to arrange an appointment for the board member and the executive director to visit her friend at the friend's home. The prospect realizes that the meeting has been called to discuss a philanthropic contribution, but no particulars were discussed on the phone (as is proper).

How Should You Ask?

If you are the board member or executive director, are you prepared to make the most of this meeting? The most important rule in major donor solicitation is to be yourself. Authenticity is the name of the game; as a noted fundraising consultant is fond of saying, "Be who you are, 'cause if you ain't who you are, you are who you ain't." Be genuine and create a mood that is friendly and comfortable. Since the board member already knows the prospect, it is her responsibility to set a friendly tone with introductions and questions about the prospect's family and current situation: "How's Ray doing at college?" "Did you catch that awful production of *Così* last month at the Opera House?" "I hope your Kauai condo survived the hurricane." Don't cut to the chase too quickly. Set the right mood, and move slowly but deliberately toward the task at hand. Note, too, that this preliminary conversation is a good opportunity to unearth additional information about the background of the prospect and his or her interest in the work of the nonprofit.

Once you've seen to the amenities, the board member might say something like this:

> *Lydia, we appreciate the fact that you've taken time out of your busy schedule to talk with us about the role that you might play in furthering the important work of [name of organization]. Why don't I let Hari [the executive director] fill you in on the wonderful work of [the organization] over the last few years and our exciting plans for the next two years?*

If you're Hari, keep your presentation short. Describe each facet of the organization's work in the effort to determine which area is of greatest interest to the prospect. Use an impressive statistic or two, and cite an example of a person whose life was improved immeasurably through the work of your program. If your organization doesn't lend itself to such a dramatic example, you still must demonstrate the impact of your program. Finish your presentation with a short but convincing description of the new and exciting work that your program will be doing in the next two years.

The board member should jump in here and discuss why she got involved with your organization. There's nothing like a volunteer who is a peer of the prospect to motivate that prospect to get involved. Don't depend on the executive director alone to make the sale. The active involvement of the peer board member is critically important.

If you've done your homework, you should be aware of the particular philanthropic interests of the prospect, the amount that she might be expected to contribute, and the aspect of your work that might be of the greatest interest to her. However, many nonprofits simply don't have the labor power to devote to adequate prospect research. Let's therefore assume that you know that the prospect has made generous contributions to other organizations and that a request of $25,000 would not be unreasonable. You do not, however, know which of your organization's efforts might be of interest to her.

Ask Open-ended Questions

In order to draw a bead on the interests of the prospect, ask open-ended questions. Don't say: "We need $25,000 to revamp our computer system and hire a part-time administrative assistant. Can you help out?" Do say: "Now that we've described the goals and projects of our organization, what questions might we answer?" (The only exception here is if your research has indicated that the only item that might be of interest to the prospect is, say, computers.)

If you ask open-ended rather than yes-or-no questions, you stand a far better chance of involving the prospect and finding out what is on her mind.

Don't Argue, Educate

The solicitation committee must list the objections and criticisms that solicitors believe they will encounter when asking for contributions, and come up next with responses to these objections. If you take the time to conduct such an exercise before beginning your solicitations, you'll be well armed to deal with the criticisms that inevitably come your way. If the prospect has a criticism of your program or field of endeavor, don't argue; educate.

For example, if the prospect brings up the unseemly battle between the past executive director and the board that made its way into the newspapers, you shouldn't get huffy about the press butting in where it doesn't belong. Instead, as the current executive director, you might respond: "I appreciate your concern about the difficulties experienced by my predecessor. I'm pleased to say that the board has been extremely gracious and helpful to me, and I anticipate a continuing excellent relationship with them. I'd like [name of board member at this meeting] to say something about that."

Be prepared to address the most common concerns that prospects will raise. It's also useful to convince the prospect that he or she is being asked to invest in the continued success of an important nonprofit, not to donate. The prospect and the nonprofit are full partners in the effort to improve the life of the community.

Listen to the Prospect

The success of your major donor effort hinges on your ability to listen to the prospect. It is a fatal error to arrive at a major donor meeting with a script that you insist on completing, come hell or high water. Like all fundraising, major donor solicitation is an art, not a science. You must be ready to respond to the prospective donor's wants, needs, and body language. If you're primed to talk about your college's beautiful new Life Sciences building and all the prospect wants to chat about is computers and Proust, you'd better be ready to shift quickly to the critical shortage of personal computers in the French Department.

We come finally to the most sensitive moment: the dollar ask. Your research should have equipped you with at least a general idea of the amount of the prospect's contribution. Once you have focused on the area of endeavor of greatest interest to the prospect, you should say something like: "I'm excited that you've shown so much interest in our computer program. In the coming year, we anticipate spending $150,000 on computer purchases, networking, and upgrading. Might we count on you for $25,000 toward this effort?"

Ask and then shut up. If the prospect is flabbergasted by the request, you'll find out. If the prospect is pleased that you've asked for so little, you'll find out (she'll whip out her checkbook then and there, which is an unmistakable sign that you've underestimated the donor's capacity!). If the prospect needs time to think, you'll find out. Let the prospect do the talking once you've made the ask.

Close the Deal

It is critically important that you close the sale. You may get a firm yes or no at this meeting. If not, it is up to you to schedule a second meeting. Don't leave matters up in the air. It's also a good idea to bring along a packet of written material to bolster your effort. If you're not proud of your brochure or annual report, you should invest some money in producing materials that are sufficiently impressive. It's wrong to assume that unattractive and poorly printed materials will prove that your organization only spends money on programs. Your materials must be appealing and impressive if you're to catch the prospect's eye and compete successfully with other nonprofits that are pursuing your prospect.

In summary, make sure the prospect is comfortable, make your case, ask for a specific amount, and close the sale. Most important, listen to the prospect. He or she will tell you all that you need to know. Be sharp, be flexible, and you will prevail!

Resource B

Major Donor Solicitation Scripts

Making the Appointment

Don't make a solicitation by phone. Simply call the prospect to make a face-to-face appointment. Your job here is to convince the prospect that it is more invasive of his or her time to stay on the phone than it would be to meet sometime in the next two weeks at his or her convenience. You will always raise more money in person than on the phone. When you're face-to-face with a prospect, you have oral and visual cues to guide you; the visual cues can make all the difference.

You might say: "I'd enjoy getting together with you, Cody, to discuss the [name of organization] and how you might be of assistance to us. Can we meet at your office sometime next week?" (If the prospect would rather meet at a neutral site such as a restaurant, that's fine, too.)

If the prospect lives outside your geographical area, you might say: "I'll be passing through [name of town or area] next week, Patsy, and I was hoping I might drop by to discuss [name of organization] and how you might assist us."

If the prospect is hesitant to meet, smooth the way by acknowledging his or her concerns: "I realize that the business climate is far from ideal, Luis, but I still hope you can spare a few minutes to hear about the important work of the [name of organization]."

The Dollar Ask

There are two schools of thought about asking the prospect for a contribution. The first contends that it is safer and more lucrative to let the prospect bring up the issue, as in this sample dialogue. We assume in this dialogue that the prospect already knows the cost of the entire project for which he or she is being approached.

Prospect: Well, I know that you're here to talk about money. How much do you need from me?

Solicitor: As we discussed earlier, outfitting the new science laboratory will cost $450,000. What portion of this amount would you consider contributing?

According to a fundraising consultant of this first school, the prospect will more often than not name a figure higher than the solicitor first had in mind. If the figure named is significantly lower than the solicitor had hoped for, he or she might say, "I appreciate your interest, but it is critically important at this stage that we pursue larger gifts. Might you consider a gift over three years that totals [three times what the prospect suggested]?"

The second, and more common, school of thought assumes that the solicitor will articulate a dollar range. The ask in this case might go like this:

Solicitor: Each member of our board has pledged to make a contribution to the extent of his or her capability. I will be making a $35,000 gift. Might we expect the same contribution from you?

Or:

Solicitor: I'm excited about your interest in our activities. As you know, we need a total of $450,000 for the science lab. Will you consider a contribution of $35,000?

Or:

Solicitor: A benchmark gift of $35,000 would get our campaign off to a great start. Will you consider such a contribution?

A Sample Major Gift Solicitation Script

(SCENE: The thirty-fourth floor of the downtown office of CARMEN MEGABUX, an obscenely successful securities trader and occasional philanthropist. CARMEN is greeting RAY SAVIOR, an old school friend who has requested a few minutes with CARMEN to talk about the Happy County Independent Living Center. RAY serves on the center's board of directors and plans to ask CARMEN for a major gift.)

Carmen: Ray, this is a pleasure! I haven't seen you since Dick and I ran into you and Emily at the bar during that horrible production of *Tosca* last fall.

Ray: That's right, Carmen. Not a great night at the opera, though it was certainly good to run into you. By the way, how are the kids?

Carmen: Well, Brad's in his second year at State U. and doesn't care about anything but computers and basketball. And Cindy's a real handful—fourteen going on nineteen, if you know what I mean, and I think you do. And how about your little darlings?

Ray: It's amazing the trouble that two-year-old twins can get into. Last week, Danny and Darlene decided that Kippy's dog food was preferable to their spaghetti. So they got down on the floor, and . . . but I'll spare you the details.

Carmen: Thank you. So tell me, my friend, what can I do for you?

Ray: Well, Carmen, as I mentioned on the phone last week, I've been a member of the Happy County Independent Living Center's board of directors for the past three and a half years. The center does incredible work on behalf of people with disabilities throughout Happy County, particularly people with little or no income. I'd like to talk to you about the center's programs, about our goals for the next couple of years, and about how you might help out.

Carmen: OK, Ray, though I warn you, business was off a little last year, and I've already got quite a few philanthropic commitments.

Ray: I appreciate that, Carmen, but do let me tell you about some of the achievements of the center. Founded twenty years ago, the center is staffed almost entirely by physically disabled people who provide counseling, services, and advocacy on behalf of other physically and developmentally disabled individuals. The staff of twelve includes two people with vision problems, one person with profound hearing loss, five people in wheelchairs, and four people without disabilities.

Carmen: It's good to hear that these people aren't just sitting home collecting government checks.

Ray: That's right. Last year, the center served over two thousand disabled Happy County residents through their programs, which include counseling for newly disabled people, job placement for the majority of disabled folks who are able to work, assistance in locating attendants to work for those disabled folks who are intent on remaining in their own homes but need help, a van transportation service to take people shopping and to doctors' appointments, advocacy efforts to ensure that local governments understand the needs of disabled folks, and a large selection of classes and recreational activities.

Carmen: Whew. That's quite a list. Is there really much of a demand for this kind of help?

Ray: You'd be amazed. There are over sixteen thousand disabled adults in Happy County, so as good a job as the center is doing, there are still thousands of people who haven't been helped.

Carmen: What about disabled kids? I saw the most darling photograph of a five-year-old girl in a wheelchair in last week's issue of *Parade*.

Ray: Well, it turns out that there are quite a few programs in the county that offer services to disabled children. Therefore, the center decided to turn its attention exclusively to adults.

Carmen: You mentioned the van program; tell me a little more about that.

Ray: It's probably no surprise to you that disabled folks have an awfully hard time getting around. While some buses and trains are accessible, many aren't, and most disabled people can't drive and can't afford chauffeurs.

Carmen: Don't tell me about chauffeurs! I'm on my fourth one in five years! Completely undependable.

Ray: I'm sure. Anyway, the center's van is available to take disabled folks from anywhere in Happy County to important appointments and on errands. Reservations generally have to be made three or four days ahead of time. The van picks people up at their homes, deposits them at their appointments, and is standing by for the trip home.

Carmen: A great program. Maybe I should use it myself. Well, it does appear that there's a need for the center, but don't my tax dollars pay for this sort of thing already?

Ray: Unfortunately not. The center's budget this year was $1.2 million. Only 30 percent of that comes from government sources. The rest must be raised privately.

Carmen: Sounds like you've got a serious fundraising job ahead of you. Tell me, Ray, what's your interest in all this? You're not disabled . . . at least not as far as I know.

Ray: Well, Carmen, I got interested in disability issues when my sister had a daughter who was born with Down's syndrome. Before I got to know Kelly, I thought that the best that could be done for disabled people would be to house them in institutions where their needs would be looked after. Well, Kelly turned out to be a great kid—lively, loving, and certainly not someone who should be locked away. So when a friend of mine at the office told me about one of the center's events, I decided to drop by.

Carmen: I can understand your interest, Ray. My next-door neighbor—who's also one of my closest friends—contracted multiple sclerosis two years ago. She's a real fighter, and I wouldn't be surprised if she licks it! Ray, it's good to hear that you're still out there fighting the good fight, but I really don't know if I can help. You must realize that I already make substantial contributions to Doctors' Hospital, the Happy Valley Ballet, and the ASPCA. How can I add another program to the list?

Ray: Carmen, you're to be commended for doing as much philanthropic work as you already do. All I can say is that the work of the center is crucial, the demand is increasing, and we have to raise funds from friends like you if we're to survive and prosper.

Carmen: Let's get down to brass tacks, Ray. How much are you looking for from me?

Ray: Carmen, I was hoping for a contribution of $50,000.

Carmen (jaw drops): $50,000!? Ray, you must be joking! You must know that the securities business took a tumble last year, and me with it. I can hardly afford the upkeep on our summer house at Lucerne. Really, that's out of the question.

Ray: I'm sorry that business was off last year, Carmen, though the center would still appreciate your help. You mentioned earlier that you were interested in the van program. How about a contribution of $35,000 toward the purchase and upkeep of the second van that the center plans to buy before the end of next year?

Carmen: Well, I'll have to talk it over with Dick, and you know how he gets about "layabouts" and "Communists." By the way, Ray, are you making a contribution to the center?

Ray: Yes, I am, Carmen. I gave $5,000 this year for the second year in a row. Also, did you know that our old classmate Jerry Crandall gave $40,000 to the center last month?

Carmen: Crandall! That meathead! How he ever succeeded in the restaurant business is beyond me! Still, I'd hate to let that guy outshine me. Look, Ray, I'll talk to my husband and I'll see what we can do.

Ray: I really appreciate that, Carmen. Let me leave you with a copy of the center's annual report and their plan for the next two years. I'll give you a call a week from Monday to see if I can answer any more questions.

Carmen: Sounds good to me. And give those twins of yours a big hug from me. Bye!

Index